Money
Magic

Money Magic

Praveen Chadha

SRISHTI PUBLISHERS & DISTRIBUTORS
64-A, Adhchini
Sri Aurobindo Marg
New Delhi 110 017

First published by Srishti Publishers & Distributors in 2001

ISBN 81-87075-32-5
Rs. 145.00

Cover Design by Creative Concept
40/223 C R Park
New Delhi 110 019

All the incidents, characters, utterances etc. in this book are a figment of the author's imagination. Any resemblance with anyone living or dead is purely coincidental.

Printed and bound in India by
Saurabh Print-O-Pack
A-16, Sector IV, Noida

Dedicated

to

The Loving Memory

of

My Mother

Late Mrs Omi Chadha

Who

Passed Away

On

24th October 2000.

Index
Money Magic

CHAPTER One
What is Money

It is everybody's sweetheart
and due to it people even part.

It travels from home to home
and it is never anybody's own.

It sometimes does a wonder
and sometimes brings a thunder.

It has the taste of honey
and it's got to be your money.

Money took birth to bring an end to the barter system. The barter system was a practice by which people changed one asset for another or parted with an asset in settlement of a debt. At the time when the barter system existed, there could have been differences amongst people. Such differences could have arisen due to the difference in the importance and value of assets exchanged. One person could have felt cheated out of a barter deal whereas the other could have felt elated. Money was introduced by mankind to bring about uniformity in the yardstick required to value items for the purposes of exchange.

Though the earlier system of barter was abolished, even now it continues to exist and floats in the medium of money.

From dawn to dusk, from day to day, from month to month and from year to year we need money. To survive from one moment to the next, we need money. To travel through time we need food, clothing and shelter that can reach us only with the help of money. When we turn the pages of history we see the role that money has all along played in the lives of people. As one generation has passed to another, the importance of money has increased. Money, therefore, has an increasing role in our lives. This is because of inflation, invention and competition, which have multiplied manifold with the efflux of time. Though money does not have any life in itself it can even end the life of both you and me.

Right from birth to death, everybody requires money at every stage of life. It is the heartthrob of every heart. Money lives in the heart of everybody right from the niggard to the magnanimous. It dwells in the heart of the rich and the poor, the good and the bad, the black and the white, the pious and the sanctimonious, the ugly and the beautiful, the victor and the vanquished and so on and so forth. It is only the importance that different people hold for money, which varies, from person to person, which ranges from the insatiable to the content. It is indeed ironical that even those who ostracize themselves and pull themselves out of the rat race for money still need money. In these circumstances, there is an unavoidable need for money that is essentially encountered by everybody.

Money is like a Giant Wheel that we get to see at a fair. We can see people paying money to purchase tickets so that they can ride in the Giant Wheel. Likewise, to earn money, one has to spend money. The Giant Wheel places different people in different positions. Similarly money determines the different social standings of different persons. We can see some people atop the Giant wheel, some at the bottom of it, some at the middle positions and some midway between the middle and either the top or the bottom. Likewise money divides people into rich, poor and the middle class. The middle class is again divided into the upper middle class and the lower middle class. We see people getting into the Giant Wheel. This is akin to people who embark into the process of earning money. People at the bottom of the Giant Wheel anxiously wait for their turn to reach the top. Likewise the poor and the middle class also look forward to becoming rich. Some people get pleasure in swinging in the Giant Wheel while others get pain in doing so. Similarly money also makes people both happy and unhappy. Most people enjoy being at the topmost position in the Giant Wheel while some feel scared after having reached this position. Likewise most people are thrilled and delighted when they become rich while some people feel scared after they become rich. The Giant Wheel takes people from the top to the bottom and vice versa. Similarly it is money that makes the rich people poor and the poor people rich. However there is one major difference between the Giant Wheel and money. The Giant Wheel stops from time to time but Money never stops performing its activities. The comparison of the Giant Wheel with money illustrates how money is an integral part and parcel of our lives.

Money gets people accommodation, business, clothes, diamonds, food etc. It is for this reason that money does not mean just the currency notes and coins but includes everything that comes to us with its help. Cars, clothes, food, fineries, houses are all the different forms of money as all of them are money's worth. Some people wrongly feel that money means only currency notes and forget to include in its definition the items that can be acquired by it.

As God is there in everything, he is also there in money. Different people worship God in different names. Likewise people worship money and also give it different names. The names that different countries give their money are different. Some countries call their money Rupee, some call it Pound Sterling, some call it Dollar, some call it Yen and some frankly call it Francs. Irrespective of how we have christened our money, we need to remember that as God dwells in money, it is surely something sacred. It is for this reason that we must never ever put money to unholy use.

Money is just a means of living. At no cost should we make it the end of our living. We should see that we make money to live and we do not live to make money. We must remember that there is much more to life than just money.

Wealth in the true sense of the word has several components, money being just one of them. The other components include happiness, a clear conscience, the feeling of satisfaction that we have used our riches and resources for others, a good health, a good reputation and good relationships. Whilst we focus on making money, we also need to focus on earning the other components of true wealth. At the end of the day it is our deeds and not our money that are remembered. The body reaches its end but the soul continues to live. After our death any amount of money is powerless and useless to help our soul.

CHAPTER Two
Why Do We Need Money

We need money because it enables us to :-

- Meet our basic needs of food, clothes and shelter.
- Take care of our health.
- Solve our problems in a crisis.
- Acquire educational qualifications.
- Improve and increase our confidence level.
- Improve our lifestyle.
- Bring safety and security in our future.
- Get us respect and recognition in the society.
- Change peoples' perception about us.
- Learn lessons out of life.
- Ensure that nobody takes us for granted.
- Get us more money.

CHAPTER Three

What Money Does

MONEY:-

afoots ambitious actions.
bullies big businessmen.

creates complicated conditions.
defeats dishonest dacoits.

excuses erring elements.
fetches frightenings figures.

groans gasping guards.
hides horrible hearts.

irks irrational idiots.
jeers jealous jokers.

louders lousy listeners.
makes mysterious mistakes.

pacifies painful pangs.
reverses rude remarks.

sometimes sprinkles sadness.
voices various vows.
worries wicked women.

It makes old people look young.
And its praises are always sung.

It makes some people conceited.
And it makes some defeated.

It makes the dying come out alive.
And it makes the successful thrive.

It makes people change their side.
And it forces some to commit suicide.

It makes people dance on their toes.
And it turns friends into foes.

It makes everyone run in its rate race.
And sometimes results in a court case.

It makes people strengthen their loyalty.
And it makes scientists invent for royalty.

It makes the wrong people feel that they are right.
And it makes loose tongues tight.

Money is that wondrous creation of Man, which keeps reminding him of God. It is a bridge that connects God with mankind. It is one of the several lines of communication between God and mankind. It is due to money that time and again we keep remembering God. Money is one of the many modes through which God sends either his blessing or his retribution. When we crave for money we remember God. When we lose money we remember God. When people make money many of them forget God but some continue to remember him. Those who never remembered God, start remembering him because of money. Sometimes money related incidents scratch our soul and awake the Lord sleeping in us. We can hear people saying " Thank God" or "God is great " when money makes them happy. On the other hand, we can hear people saying "Oh, My God" or " Lord have mercy " when money makes them unhappy. Sometimes we see very stingy people making generous offerings to God. They feel that such generosity shall make their dreams come true. This is one of the many doings of money.

It is a blunt and bitter truth that in this materialistic world the one with money is the one who is respected. People feel that sooner or later a moneyed man may be of some help to them. It is probably for this reason that a moneyed man is respected. In the materialistic world money is considered to be a parameter of success. The more the money a person possesses, the more he/she is considered to be successful and the more is the respect he/she gets. It is surprising that the moneyed people get respect even without asking for it. The moneyed man commands respect without demanding for it. Having received respect regularly, a stage comes when the rich start expecting respect. When the expected respect is not forthcoming, then their hearts burn with anger. When the moneyed are not moneyed anymore, they are by and large not respected anymore. It is a hard and harsh fact that when money comes, it brings respect with it and when it goes it carries away the respect it had brought. A rich man may feel that people respect him but he is sadly mistaken. It is not he but it is his money that is respected.

Some people who live in abject poverty keep suffering endlessly. They do not possess money that could have met even their basic requirements of food, clothes and shelter. It is for this reason that their lives are filled up with sorrows and sufferings. They are treated shabbily wherever they go. The reason is that their misfortune reaches their destination before them. They keep getting insulted time and again but are unable to protect themselves against insult. The reason is that they have very little say in their own lives. Their existence becomes their punishment. At times some of them wish that they died so that their suffering could also die with them. Some such people even change their religion so that they can reduce their misery. Their new religion gives them a new lease of life. Sometimes after changing their religion they are given employment. This gets them money, which in turn gets them food, clothing and shelter. At times their new religion does not provide them employment but provides them periodically with food and clothes. Some such people not only change their religion but also their integrity. The fire in their stomach burns up their ideals of life.

Sometimes we come across two people who cannot stand the sight of each other. The two do not wish to look at one another. Each one is filled up with hatred for the other. It is surely surprising to see the two working together and earning their livelihood. During the course of their work the two not only speak to one another but even cooperate with one another. Though their hearts hate one another, money makes their hearts beat together. It is amazing that money unites even enemies and makes them work shoulder to shoulder. Is this not a miracle of money?

Money decides how people would remember and react to the name of the dead. When the deceased leaves behind a lot of wealth, the inheritors remember him/her with love and affection. That is a different matter that generally such love withers away with time. It is ironical that first the inherited money makes them remember the dead and then it helps them to forget the deceased. Sometimes the deceased had either disinherited someone or had cheated someone. Then those who feel aggrieved due to such disinheritance or cheating curse both themselves and the deceased. Sometimes in such situations even time does not eat up memory. That is how important money is for those who are alive and probably also for those who are dead.

The untouchables are an unfortunate lot. Their plight has always found place in the pages of history. It is surely inhuman to treat any human being as an untouchable. All of us are alike and no one is an untouchable in the true sense of the word. People who treat others as untouchables are a hypocritical lot. When it comes to money then the untouchables are treated differently. People who treat someone as an untouchable do not treat the money touched by him / her as untouchable. Even a Brahmin is more than willing to accept money from a harijan. This is how money makes the untouchables lose their untouchibility.

Life is a bed of roses with thorns in it. Money can either increase the number of roses or the number of thorns in our lives. Likewise it is with the help of money that we can generally increase either the number of roses or the number of thorns in the lives of others. Money in itself is neither good nor bad. It is we who put our money to either good or bad use. If we put our money to good use, we bring happiness and harmony in the world. On the other hand if we put money to bad use, we bring horror and hatred in the world. It is not the amount of money we have that is important, it is how we use our money that makes all the difference.

Even diametrically different occasions have one factor that converge them together. What else can that factor be but money. Money is needed both at the time of marriage and divorce. It is also needed to perform both the rituals of birth and death. Likewise divergent intentions can both be fulfilled by money. Sometimes when an employer wishes to retain an employee, the employee is encouraged to take an interest free loan from the employee. The loan is to be repaid in easy installments while the employee is in harness. Better still, the loan is to be adjusted only from the benefits accruing to the employee at the time of retirement. This means that the employee is not required to repay the loan during his/her tenure of service. Sometimes such mouth-watering offer is hard to refuse and therefore accepted by the employee. At times such loans carry a stipulation that interest shall be payable at the commercial rate with retrospective effect if and when the employee resigns from the job. These types of loans provide a golden handcuff for the employee. On the contrary if the employer wishes to terminate the services of an employee, a mutually acceptable amount of money is paid to the employee on the understanding that the employee's services shall be mutually terminated. This in common parlance is called a golden handshake. Someone had rightly said that Money makes the mare go.

A man behaved like an outright idiot in his workplace. He kept cracking cheap and childish jokes with his peers, subordinates and some superiors. While he laughed at the jokes he cracked, others laughed at him. Sometimes he bored his colleagues with stale stories about his grand parents. While his colleagues were discussing about a movie which all of them had watched together, he suddenly started saying that he was dying to eat tandoori chicken.

His colleagues reacted by smiling suggestively at one another. He attended the wedding of one of his colleagues and danced enthusiastically but disgracefully. People laughed at his clumsy manner of dancing. Sometimes while he was at work he burped loudly and drew the attention of other people. He could be seen beaming at the funeral of one his colleagues. At times he could be overheard talking to himself. He responded to "Hello" with words such as "Shut up", "Sorry" and "Thank you". Everyone at his workplace branded him as a lunatic. Some said that he needed to go for a brain scan. Some suggested that a Psychiatrist should treat him. One fine day people detected that their so called lunatic had single handedly swindled a sum of Rs 2 Crores from their company. It was then that their impression about this man took a summersault. Those who had recommended a Psychiatrist for him ate back their words. They realised that their colleague had willfully behaved in a clumsy manner to misguide them and rule out the possibility of getting caught. Those who had branded him as mad were now convinced that he was not mad but crafty and calculative. Deep in their hearts some colleagues even started respecting him. After all, sometimes what our eyes get to see and our ears get to hear is not the truth. Money had brought about a radical change in the impression people held about their so-called lunatic.

Sometimes we have a bad impression about some people without having had any direct dealing with them. Such an impression is formed on the basis of rumours about these people. Some of us strongly believe the rumours about others and think about them accordingly. At times the wrong impression we hold about such people changes completely. We vehemently confirm the same person who was written off as horrible by us to be wonderful. This happens due to the monetary help extended to us by such people at the time of need. When unexpectedly such people lend us money to get our near and dear ones operated, pay off our electricity/telephone bills to prevent disconnection, stall our dismissal from the work place, get us employment etc then we realise our folly in relying on such rumours. It is surely not wise to rely on rumours. It should be on the basis of our dealings with people that we form an opinion about them. Rumours could be a result of jealousy, settlement of old scores, wagging of loose tongues, contamination of the truth including exaggeration etc. Money can sometimes act as an eye opener and bring us closer to reality.

A man and his parents kept harassing his wife to get money from her poor widowed mother. Their persistent demands for money had made life miserable for the helpless girl. Her mother was left with no more money that could

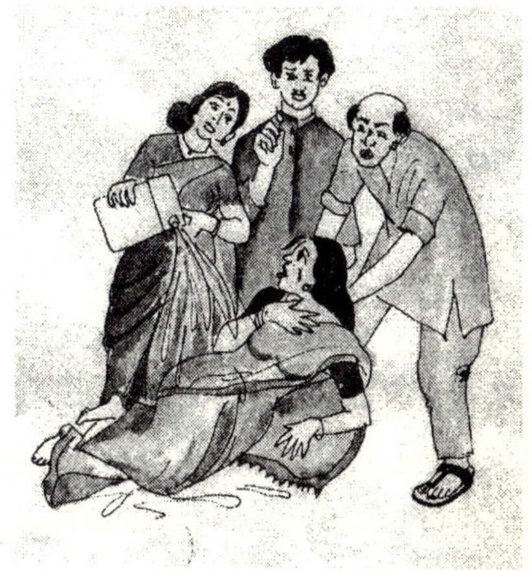

be given to the greedy people. Angered with the fact that she could get no more money from her mother, the three took drastic action. They poured kerosene on the poor girl and set her ablaze. She eventually died. The three culprits greased the palms of those who were investigating the matter. The unfortunate incident was hushed up. The murder had been committed so that the boy could marry an extremely rich girl. The marriage was solemnised. The bride had brought with her a huge amount of dowry. Besides the dowry, she also brought havoc to the family. She quarreled regularly with her in-laws. She took delight in affronting and humiliating them. She kept reminding them of their socio-economic status vis-à-vis that of her parents. In a fit of rage, she told her mother-in-law "You said that I am the spoilt child of my rich parents. Look at yourself and your family upbringing. You killed your son's wife so that you could pocket money from my parents. Is this what you have learnt from your parents?" As usual, once her husband had asked her parents for money. They gave him the money and she gave him a piece of her mind. She told him. "You are a beggar with an invisible bowl. You and your greed are discussed largely at my parent's place." She kept reminding her husband that her father had engineered his success. She brainwashed her husband against his parents. She promoted her husband's relation with her parents at the cost of his relationship with his parents. Eventually the relationship between her in-laws and their only issue vanished in the blue. The boy's parents kept comparing their daughter-in-law's horrendous behaviour with that of the good girl they had burnt. In retrospect they felt that she was both an ideal daughter-in-law and an ideal wife. It was then that they realised the gravity of the sin they had committed. Money is like a mirror; it shows us the true reflection of our innerself. It also reminds us that the world is round and we reap according to what we have sown.

Money is both a troublemaker and a troubleshooter. First it creates problems and then it solves the problems it had created. Some people take advantage of this feature of money and they make money in the bargain. Such instances include a schoolteacher regularly failing students to get tuition, a trade union leader creating a problem so that he gets his promotion and crooked in-laws making issues out of nothing so that their daughter-in-law gets them dowry. Once the student starts taking tuition from the schoolteacher, the management gives the union leader his promotion and the daughter-in-law gets the dowry, their problems disapper. Thanks to money.

A man was completely demoralised at his work place. The reason was that he had not been prometed in five years. Those who were his subordinates had become his superiors by the dint of their hard work. Initially he was not performing satisfactorily, as he was lazy. Later on he was unwilling to do any work as he knew that he would remain stagnated and static. One day his new boss summoned him for a deliberation. The man told his tale and shared his plight with his boss. His boss took up the matter with his boss. One fine day a letter was handed over to this man. He was pleased to read that he had received a double promotion and his salary was increased by 150 %. At the time of handing over the letter to him he was told that this was being done only on an experimental basis. He was also told that thereafter he had to work really hard, failing which he would be dismissed. He was extremely happy. The increase in his salary helped him to fulfill those desires that had never been fulfilled. That gave him a fillip to work. Overnight the man's attitude towards his work changed. He took active interest in his work. He came to office in time and left late. Unlike before he never wasted any time in gossiping with his colleagues. He completed extremely difficult tasks with considerable ease. He finished these tasks well before time. He and his outstanding output became the talk of the office. A person who was once upon a time a lazy lump had now become a shooting star. He was cited as a good example and others were asked to follow his footsteps. His boss was pleased with him as he did not let him down. His boss's boss was pleased with his boss, as his advice had fetched fabulous results. Thanks to money that had played the role of a mammoth motivator. It had activated the passive making a hero out of a zero.

We see a closely-knit family. There is tremendous amount of love shared in the family. In sharp contrast, we see a lot of distance between the members of another family. This distance is conspicuous even when such members are sitting close to one another. It is money that is the main reason for the disparity in such situations. A poor family may not have adequate money but has no dearth of love. Lack of money binds them together. A rich family has money but this money causes distance between its members. It is money that drifts the family members apart from one another either slowly or suddenly. At times even money is hamstrung to affect the quantum of love shared in the family.

Wherever money reaches or leaves any place or person, it is always followed by change. Change follows money like a shadow and the two always keep constant company. Due to money changing hands, people experience change. Sometimes one change brought about by money brings countless consequential changes in its aftermath. The different types of changes encountered by people due to money could be in their actions and attitudes, beauty and boldness, creativity and craftiness, dependability and desirability and of course in their wickedness and wisdom. Such changes could be either for the better or for the worse. Sometimes a change that seems to be for the better is actually for the worse and vice versa. It is our experiences in the future which prove whether a change has been for the better or for the worse. After all, amongst other factors money too makes life a mystery. It is time that ends this mystery and shows us the reality.

Money gives rise to several forces which are self-cancelling. It is a magical wand that can cause both the birth and death of several aspects of life. These aspects include ambition and arrogance, blessing and bickering, grouse and grief, holocaust and hatred, love and luxury, pride and prosperity, splendour and simplicity and of course so on and so forth. Such aspects whether good or bad are interwoven into our lives for good.

In the journey of life it is money that transports us from one state to another. Such a change in condition affects our appearance, attitude, lifestyle and preferences. It keeps changing people off and on. Sometimes money changes people beyond recognition. It moves people from meekness to audacity, ignorance to education, simplicity to sophistication and undoubtedly from rejection to acceptance! Money is the crucial factor that determines how we would describe our journey of life. Some describe it as a jaunt, some as a nightmare, some as satisfactory and others describe it as unsatisfactory.

With its power, money reduces the distance between people who are positioned in different places. This is due to the aeroplanes, computers, fax machines, postal services, telephones and satellite televisions which all exist due to money. It connects countries with the help of its network thereby enabling them to meet their objectives. All these people have different objectives in their lives. Though their objectives are different, they all have one objective that is common. This objective is that of reaching the destination of money.

When we see the givings and misgivings of money,

we rediscover the importance of the role it plays in our lives. The givings or misgivings of money can result in astonishing arrogance, broken barriers, cunning cousins, dead dogs, eager entrepreneurs and fluctuating fortunes. Some more givings and misgivings of money include hysterical heights, increasing insults, pregnant pauses, ruptured relations, scurvy statements, tough talk and even lost lives.

Money is responsible for causing several consequences, which could be either for the better or for the worse. The miracle of money makes people applaud and assault, belittle and beautify, cry and calculate, dismiss and dance, elite and educated, fight and frown and of course good and generous. It's magic also makes people detest and rest, mediate and retaliate, mourn and groan, earn and yearn, jeer and cheer and undoubtedly eat and beat. Of course there is certainly certain amount of contribution we make in reaching ourselves to such consequences.

Money makes the wheel of life move differently for different people. For the fortunate few who have the blessings of money it moves in the correct clockwise direction. For the others it moves in the opposite direction and life treats them unkindly. Mankind gave birth to money, which it in turn has made mankind its slave. At this moment while you are reading this book, man continues to remain a captive in the hands of his own creation. Without having any life in itself, money controls the lives of people. Perhaps this is one of the reasons why some people worship the Goddess of Money.

MONEY brings tears in the eyes.
MONEY makes us listen to sighs.
MONEY lost makes people frown.
MONEY makes reputations drown.

CHAPTER Four

The Colour of Money

Quite often we listen to people referring to money as either "Black Money" or " White Money". White money is that money which has been disclosed to the tax authorities. Unless such money is exempt from tax, it has been taxed. The society honours such money by painting it virgin white. On the other hand, Black Money is that money which has not been disclosed to the tax authorities. Consequently it has not been taxed. The "Society" unwittingly condemns such money by painting it with the darkest of all colours.

For many people the value of money is far more important than its colour. Such people attach paramount importance to the uses and utilities of money and no importance to its colour or character. These people feel that whether money is black or white, it continues to be money. They feel that the purchasing power of money hardly changes with its colour. Some such people keep suppressing their income from the Government thereby amassing black money. By doing so they cheat their motherland. In sharp contrast to this, there are honest citizens of their motherland who never suppress their income from the Government. They honestly and wisely keep paying tax on their income. These people do not choose to blacken their faces with black money.

The exchequer of a country is its financial strength. Our taxes are our contribution to our nation. When we evade taxes, we deprive the nation of its dues. By doing so we not only cause damage to its present position but also to the face of its future. As sons of the soil we have a duty to discharge. It is the duty of being loyal to our country. Our loyalty includes our honesty in paying our taxes.

By not paying our taxes honestly we create bottlenecks and barriers for the Government. We cause hardship to the Government in meeting its expenditure, both planned and unplanned. Such misconduct on our part disables the Government from meeting its objectives effectively and efficiently. The Government uses our contributions of taxes for various purposes. The key purposes for which the Government uses our taxes comprise of :

- Safe guarding the barriers and borders of our country.
- Equipping our country with adequate and appropriate armaments.
- Training our soldiers for our safety.
- Improving the image of our country in the international arena.
- Research to ensure optimal use of the resources of our country.
- Building roads and bridges for our convenience and comfort.
- Implementation of plans aimed at eradicating poverty.
- Imparting education to the poor.

When we see the purposes that our taxes serve, we discover the importance of our contribution to the exchequer. Those who circumvent their tax liability by resorting to dubious means ought to realise the damage they are causing their own country.

People possess black money thinking that it shall bring them safety and security. Ironically such money brings them tension and trauma. People are scared that the Tax Authorities might unearth their black money. If that happens they would be taken to task for having evaded their taxes. Such constant tension undermines their health. If that happens then their black money is spent on medicare. Some people alienate their assets that were purchased out of black money. This is done to ensure that they are not traced by the taxmen. Such assets are held in the name of their friends and relatives. At times, the legal owner asserts his/her title on such assets depriving the actual owner of the asset. Probably the legal owner feels that such assets are easy to usurp. These are some of the many misgivings of black money.

When we watch cricket matches or movies we can see the loyalty people have for their country. We also get to see the same sentiment at the time of war. All of us should ask ourselves a question. Why do we not show such loyalty when it comes to payment of our taxes?

CHAPTER Five

What Money Cannot Do

I am Money. There is a lot that I can do for you and there is little that I cannot. The little may be little, but it more than makes up for the lot. I cannot trap time in my hand as it slips away just like dry sand. I cannot bring you ease as and when you please. I cannot decide my ownership. I cannot cut my wings. I cannot stop playing hide and seek with you. I cannot buy you peace of mind. I cannot defeat the truth. I cannot justify your wrongdoing. I cannot change your past. I cannot impress you if you are an idealist. I cannot perform those miracles that can only be performed by God. I cannot forgive your sins that can only be forgiven by God. I cannot give you death that can be given only by God. After your last rites will be over, people may or may not speak about me. But they all would know that I had lived with you and you had lived with me. I cannot die with you and you shall die without me.

CHAPTER Six

Rich and Poor

The rich sometimes shamelessly rob,
leaving the poor to sob.

Some rich commit sin after sin,
leaving no hope to pin.

Some poor become rich,
throwing snobs in the ditch.

Though all human beings have the common features such as blood, bones, organs, muscles etc. their life style is never the same. This is due to money that separates all the children of God into the rich and the poor. While the rich flourish in their fortunes, the poor suffer in their starvation. Every sunrise is a new day for the rich which brings a new way of making money. On the other hand, for our poor brethren every new day is looked upon for some ray of hope. The poor live in a microcosm of their own which is looked at by some rich rascals with ridicule and repulsiveness.

Between the rich and the poor lies the middle class. This class of people are called the middle class as they are in the middle with the rich on one side and the poor on the other side. These people are like the fulcrum which balances a sew saw and are by and large envied by the poor and looked down upon by the rich. The thorns in their lives outnumber the roses. For such people meeting their ends is a Herculean task. Sacrificing one luxury or even a necessity for another is an integral part and parcel of their lives. These people crave to become rich and sometimes do make it. Such an achievement is made by hard work, sacrifice, planning, managing and sometimes by even resorting to dubious means.

While the poor hunt for food in the litterbins, the rich choose which cuisine to have. While the rich count their currency notes, the ribs of the poor unfed people can be counted. While the rich keep dogs as pets feeding them well, the poor helplessly live on the roads with the dogs. While in their distress the poor have forgotten their birthday, the rich celebrate the birthday of their pets. While the poor have pains in their belly, the rich enjoy watching belly dances. It is really so surprising that a poor man's monthly earning is less than the money spent by a rich man on a single meal. The rich and the poor live in the same world but ironically money makes their respective world divergent and different.

A rich man returned from his world tour. During his absence his servant was living in his house. Except for the drawing room, kitchen and a toilet all the other rooms of the house were locked. The master returned home and lodged a complaint with the police. He accused the servant

of doing away with a sum of Rs 3 lacs. He lied that he had left the money locked up in the cupboard, which was kept in the drawing room. The police came and interrogated the servant who was taken into custody. The police even assaulted the servant. He wept and pleaded innocent but it was all of no avail. The poor servant served a sentence for a crime that he had never committed. The poor man knew that he had been made the scapegoat. He knew that evidence had been manufactured against him. The master lodged an insurance claim and realised the money that he had never lost. On receiving the money his heart danced for joy the way a peacock dances before the arrival of the rain. The money had reimbursed him the expenditure incurred on his world tour. The money had brought with it the crying curses of the innocent servant. The man had thought that the servant was too poor to either defend himself or do any harm to the master. The innocent servant felt that the guilty master had taken full advantage of his poverty and gone scot-free.

Years rolled on. The poor servant had been freed. One day he went to buy groceries from a shop. All of a sudden he saw the picture of that monstrous master on a packet that was made by using an old newspaper. The shopkeeper read out the news to the servant. Another domestic servant who was working with the master had killed the master. Using a cycle chain he had strangled the master to death. The master had roped that servant into a similar situation. He had failed to succeed in trying his old tricks. After all, every day is not a Sunday. History had done its justice. There are some rich people who feel that the poor are unprivileged or under-privileged. Such people do not realise that the poor are actually over-privileged. This is because the poorer a man is, the closer he is to God.

It is really unfortunate that one gets to hear of daughters belonging to a poor family committing suicide. This is a consequence flowing out of the poverty of their parents and the persistent demands for money in the form of dowry by certain greedy people. Such people are the family members of the boy who has been identified as the prospective son-in-law. The daughters who see their poor parents depressed due to their failure to get a matrimonial match for them feel guilty of being born as females. Sometimes in their plight and frustration the parents curse, abuse and even beat up the daughters. Such instances recur and the frequency sometimes depends upon the number of failures emanating out of marriage negotiations. This drives the girls to face dire consequences including sexual harassment by some perverted men and sometimes even the chastity is in jeopardy. The future is looked at with complete disillusionment and the desire to live is lost forever. When all the daughters are of marriageable age then each one has the same feeling almost simultaneously. Where there is an age difference between the daughters, then the younger ones are sure of facing similar consequences in the future. The girls come to a decision of committing suicide and more often than not they resort to the same means. Lives are lost in the family and the hearts of the poor parents are broken. Really this is one of the many misgivings of being poor. Thanks to the money mongers who keep dying for dowry failing to realise that the qualities of the girl are far more important than the dowry brought by her.

Children attending school are asked to wear the same uniform. The uniform is aimed at not discriminating the rich students from the poor ones. Children are a form of God. Unlike we grown ups, the disparity in riches is largely unknown to them and is not reflected in their behaviour. Of course poor children who work for a livelihood are aware of the pains of being poor and the pleasures of being rich. More often than not, such children are overworked and underpaid. The other children are usually unaware of such realities. Of course as they start growing up they start becoming aware of the tragedies outpoured by poverty and realize the pleasures of being rich. This is a way of the world which no matter hard we try, we cannot eradicate.

CHAPTER Seven

Attributes Needed to Make Money Honestly

Integrity: Money makes many people lose their integrity. Our integrity is exceedingly important. At no cost should we lose it. Remember that it is easy to lose our integrity for the sake of money. But once we have lost our integrity, it is impossible for us to buy it back. Any amount of money cannot find integrity that has been lost. Sooner or later the one who loses his integrity is bound to lose his reputation. It is only a matter of time. In the long run it is our integrity which gets us that money which brings us joy. Such money is also relatively more permanent in nature. On the other hand, money, which is ill gotten, carries with it the curse of those who have been wronged. Which is why it is bound to cause sorrow to its owner. After all, the means never justifies the end.

Observation Power: If we keep our eyes and ears open we are bound to discover some route by which we can make money. To make money we need to see how others make money. And then we should examine if we can adopt such means or not. Advertisements and announcements in the newspapers, magazines, radio, television and Internet provide vital information. This information can be used to make money. It is our observation power that helps us to explore possibilities and exploit opportunities. We have to be vigilant and carry out a search for good opportunities, which could prove to be golden.

Introspection: We need to look into ourselves to discover our strengths and weaknesses. Others who know us could help us to know ourselves better. For this we need to remember the compliments or criticisms we have received in the past. We need to match our profession with our inclinations and interests keeping in mind our resources. We need to look at our past without restricting ourselves to our failures. In the past even if we had achieved success we could have still made some mistakes which should not be repeated in the future. We need to put questions to ourselves. These questions should be thoughtfully chosen and honestly answered. Remember that dishonest answers would tantamount to cheating us and not others. We should look at the possibility of choosing a vocation, which suits our lifestyle. In the alternative we can consider changing our lifestyle.

Imagination and Anticipation: We need to visualize situations that could arise while we carry out our moneymaking activities. The bottlenecks and ifs & buts should be studied and anticipated. We need to survey situations to determine what leads to what. We ought to remember that foresight comes only with insight. We should plan remedial measures to rectify any adverse consequences that may come our way. Remember that our thoughts always get translated to reality. Hence our thought process must be disciplined and distinct.

Tact and Tolerance: Nothing comes in this world without a price. This particularly holds good for money. When it comes to moneymaking we need to have control over our emotions. Our feelings cannot be vented out impulsively if we wish to reach the destination of money. We need to be tactful to say the right kind of things at the right time to the right persons in the right manner. Remember that the presentation of our grievances is directly related to their acceptance. We need to study and understand who listens to whom. This will help us to achieve our objectives. We have to respond and react by the head and not by the heart alone. Everyone is sentimental and we should never take anyone for granted. If we do so, we may be in for a rude surprise. Anger is the enemy of tact and tolerance. While tact and tolerance help us to achieve our objectives, anger prevents us from doing so.

Being an Extrovert: Meeting people and interacting with them helps us in making money. It enhances the ways and means by which we can make money. People bring with them opportunities, ideas, references, resources etc which can guide us to reach the destination of money. Increasing our social circle increases our chances of making money. It also has an impact on the quantum of the money we can make.

Time Management: We need to determine and decide how and when we waste our productive time. For few days we need to ask ourselves whether we are wasting our time. During such days time spent by us on different activities should be determined. Extra time spent on any activity should be identified and cut down. Likewise we must identify idle time that is wasted by us doing nothing and we need to eliminate the same. We also need to think how such time can be cut down and diverted for productive purposes. One such purpose could be that of making money. Undesirable people who waste our time should be kept at bay.

Good Health: To make money we need to constantly take care of our health. Food, Sleep and Exercise have a direct impact on our health. Hereditary sicknesses should be kept at bay by taking adequate caution. We need to remember that prevention is better than cure. Our health is bound to affect both the quality and the quantity of our work. It is difficult for a sick person to bring the desired results in the desired time. His health stands in the way of his performance. At the work front people begin to have negative preconceived notions about a sick person. Even if the output of his work is good both in terms of quality and quantity, colleagues and competitors begin to question his future output. Bad health becomes a barrier in the way of our growth.

Sacrifice: Money requires us to make a series of sacrifices to reach it. The more one is willing to sacrifice, the more is the possibility of one's making money. For the purpose of making money, different people make different types of sacrifices at different points of time. Such sacrifices include the separation from loved ones, the loss of mental peace, the job hazards and withstanding insults. Other sacrifices include the loss of sleep, disturbing dreams and even the deterioration or death of relationships. All the people who possess money have at sometime or the other surely made some sacrifice or the other to possess it. The million-dollar question is to what extent such sacrifices should be made. One needs to know where to strike the balance.

Determination: This is one of the many keys to making money. At no cost should failure demoralise us. We should become more determined as we experience failure. We should try to find out the causes for our failure. We need to remember that the cause is almost always responsible for the consequence. The causes for the failure must be eradicated so that the consequences are desirable. Every failure makes us more experienced. Our experiences including our failures should be used to achieve success. Seldom do our efforts reap results in the first attempt. One must remember to see the future of a victory hiding in every failure.

Confidence: We need to have confidence in ourselves. We must believe in ourselves. When we believe in ourselves, then only will others believe in us. We should believe that we are second to none. Repeatedly reminding ourselves that we can do it will actually make us do it. Remember that both lack of confidence and overconfidence harm us. Both are instrumental in making us commit mistakes.

Good Opportunities: Such opportunities knock on everybody's door. Some people avail of them, some people are unaware of their arrival and some let them go. Those who do not cash on these opportunities regret after these have come and gone. We need to be alert and study all the opportunities that come our way. That will help us to pick and choose the good opportunities. Just waiting for good opportunities to arrive is not enough. We need to search for good opportunities so that we can make money. If we do so then subsequently we are bound to bless ourselves.

New Skills: New skills are needed to improve and increase our chances of earning money. We need to remember that our new skills will bring us new sources of income. Thoughtfully and with farsight with we need to identify these new skills. We need to examine and evaluate the monetary benefit we would derive on acquiring such skills. Thereafter we should proceed to acquire such skills.

Flexibility: If we wish to make money we ought to be flexible. Being rigid is bound to hinder and hamper our moneymaking mechanism. That in turn will adversely affect the amount of money we make. We need to adapt and adjust ourselves with changing environments. We need to be receptive to the views of other people.

Training: If the vocation chosen by us requires any training then we must acquire the same. But first we need to carry out a research regarding the institutions that offer the same. We need to make a comparative study of the various alternatives and then proceed with the course. We must compare the quality of training, duration of the course, the cost thereof and the timings vis-a-vis our suitability. We must try to make the best of the training, as that will be of immense help to us in the future.

Move with Time: As time passes by old techniques of making money start becoming obsolete. New techniques are needed in the new era. We need to keep ourselves abreast with changing times. If we fail to do so, we would be lagging behind in the rat race of making money. We are bound to lose money if we get antiquated.

CHAPTER Eight
How People Make Money

Making money is not synonymous with earning money. This is due to the fact that in this world those who possess money have not always earned it. Besides earning money the other means of making money include begging, betting, blackmailing, deceiving, extorting, inheriting, and of course lying. These ways of making money by means other than earning are only illustrative and not exhaustive. It is quite possible that I have forgotten to include some way by which you or someone known to you has made money. That being the case, you would agree with me that it is impossible to keep stock of all the ways by which people make money.

There are a plethora of factors that determine the manner in which people make money. Such factors include the fortune of the family in which one is born, one's inherent talents, one's likes or dislikes, the parental profession or business and the scope to go in for further studies. Other factors include the impact of one's past experiences, the influence of one's company, the responsibility on one's shoulders and also one's upbringing. The moneymaking method also depends on one's integrity. We do also get to see people changing their rectitude, which makes them change their way of making money. Attending the knock of good opportunity on our door also makes us adopt a new way of making money. The good opportunity need not necessarily be good in the true sense of the word. This is due to the reason that an opportunity, which is good in terms of money, may be bad in terms of values. After all in the process of making money people do sometimes earn a bad name. Though the bad name is earned, the money is not always earned?

A man started losing the hair on his head. Little by little he had lost a lot of hair. He consulted many people about this problem. He had exhausted all his efforts in trying to grow hair on his head. He reached a stage when he had very little hair left on his head. One day as usual he looked at himself in the mirror. Thoughts passed through his mind and kept him busy thinking. He shaved off the little hair that was left on his head and he became bald. Thereafter he started offering his head to advertisers for a price. They engaged both him and his head and paid him for the same. He took advantage of what people had called his disadvantage. After all it is our attitude which gets us our money.

An extremely successful insurance agent was asked how he had embarked into the insurance business. The gentleman replied that he got the idea on reading the Income tax Act. He added that the Act mentioned about the tax treatment to be adopted for incomes from different types of business and professions. It also mentioned how tax should be deducted at source differently from people carrying out different commercial activities. The different businesses and professions mentioned about in the Act included poultry farming, interior decoration, shipping business, civil construction, hotel business etc. Those who read the Income Tax Act read it to know the provisions of the law. It probably does not occur to most of us to read it from the angle that this insurance agent had read it. He had earned a fortune out of the profession he had entered into, due to his right perspective. After all when we view things with a creative perspective, we are bound to benefit.

For the sake of making money some media persons publish tall stories by blowing real stories out of proportion. Fiction, falsity and flavour are added by them to incidents to make them sound sensational and stimulating. The insatiable inquisitiveness of the readers is fed with articles which are either poorly researched or contain inaccurate information. At times an unfortunate incident is distastefully and disgracefully described to create the wrong feelings amongst the readers. For instance the incident of the gang rape of a woman reads like a pulp fiction. Far from creating revulsion or rage amongst the male readers, such articles sexually arouse them. Really such a potboiler should boil our blood. Some newspapers declare the dying to be dead. Some newspapers slander celebrities and invade their privacy. Some newspapers ceremonise scandals to make money. When the aggrieved takes them to task, they try to either neutralise or mitigate the damage by publishing either an apology or a corrigendum. At times the victims carry the matter to the court, making the money mongers fork out money.

Disgusted and disappointed by the disparaging remarks about her broken teeth, a girl visited a dentist. She had several sittings with the dentist. During the course of the treatment the girl felt interested in working as a dentist. She took training in dentistry and started practicing. As time passed, she became a famous dentist and had earned substantial money out of her profession. It was then that she felt indebted to those people who had ridiculed her for her ugly teeth. In trying to hurt her sentiments temporarily these people had done her permanent good. She had gained by paying heed to the criticism about her teeth. After all, if we handle constructive criticism correctly we could gain in the bargain.

Over the decades though the morality of our movies have deteriorated distressingly, their popularity have multiplied manifold. Shamelessness is shown largely on the screen. Some people feel that the more the shamelessness in the movie, the greater are the chances of it becoming a hit. Cheap lyrics carrying words with either double meaning or objectionable outcome are heard in the songs of movies. One gets to watch actors and actresses performing pelvic movements while doing their deplorable dances. In the stories of some movies the bad become richer and the good get poorer. All this is done to meet the needs of the masses and not that of the classes. After all it is the masses and not the classes that determine the commercial success of a movie. Some moviemakers take recourse to such a course of action so that they can merrily make money. They fail to realise that by doing so they are causing severe damage to our society. After all our movies do overwhelmingly influence our people.

In life we come across people who are well educated but do not use their education to make a living. This represents an engineer running his family business of garment manufacture, a doctor acting in movies, a computer specialist carrying on the business of estate agency and so on and so forth. Sometimes when the business of such an engineer, doctor, computer specialist etc runs into rough weather, his education comes to his rescue. It is then that their educational skills are utilised to earn a living. After all education is one of the many keys to earn money. It can be used at any time to open the door for money. Moreover it has been rightly said that education is that asset which cannot be damaged, robbed, lost etc. It is for this reason that education needs no insurance.

Some people are employed or engaged to solve serious problem(s) against the payment of money. Amongst such people few people hold the view that self-importance is a basic ingredient that is needed to make money. These people never solve any problem fully. They let the problem linger and keep it alive. By keeping the problem alive they keep their importance alive. Consequently they make money during the life of the problem. The amount of money that they make is directly proportional to the life of the problem. The longer the life, the more the money.

All around us we get to see people doing various jobs to earn money by honest means. Such jobs include polishing shoes, polishing floors, cleaning utensils, cleaning ears, washing clothes, stitching clothes, repairing cars and painting cars. One can also see people selling cooked food on the streets, selling vegetables in the markets and a scavenger searching the litterbins. Some people describe these jobs as menial jobs and classify them as small. The smallness actually lies in the size of their own brains. People who call such jobs small themselves do supposedly bigger jobs, which are small in terms of moral value. When it comes to making money the size of their brains expands to become big. Surely no job is small and we ought to remember that labour has a dignity, which must be respected.

Two fruit vendors would put up their stalls by the side of one another. One of them was a twenty something and the other was a forty something. The two would call out "Apples, Pineapples, Custard apples etc." The names of the fruits depended on the season. While calling out the names of the fruits that were being sold, one would raise his voice louder than the other. Though the volume of their voices was different, the names of the fruits were the same. One never sold any fruit that was not sold by the other. The fruits that were sold by both of them were always fresh. In contrast the prices at which the fruits were being sold were different. The difference was significant and so were the sales. Customers patronising the vendor who was selling the fruits cheaper felt that the other vendor was foolish. They felt that his fruits were not selling because of the price he charged. In their sneaking sympathy for him some people even voiced their view to him. In response to that, he would chuckle. He felt that he was not foolish but they were foolish. They saw only as much as they were shown. At the end of the day the two men met at a hideout. Can you take a guess as to what the two men did at the hideout? They were in cahoots with one another and shared their profits. That was how they made their money. Whenever someone is selling something at an abnormally low price there is surely something wrong somewhere.

Sometimes getting a young son of marriageable age married can also be targeted at making money. In a hurry to get dowry from the girl's relatives, the boy's parents are in a haste to get him married. If the boy hails from a rich family then only girls from rich families are generally eyed. Many people who

exploit such a situation try to make money in some form or the other in the bargain. Such people comprise of relatives from either the boy's side or the girl's side. Once the marriage is solemnised and the dowry is pocketed by the boy's parents or those who brought him up, then the responsibility of the girl is conveniently loaded on to the boy. It is then that the boy is told to face his music. The unfortunate boy who was not even settled financially and was forced to get married now feels burdened with responsibility, which was initially promised to be shared. This is one of the many ways in which people make money leaving others in the lurch. Boys should get married only when they are financially well settled. If the decision to marry is made in haste then largely they would be repenting at leisure

It really touches anybody's heart when one spots a poor person earning money instead of begging for it. Employing oneself in a manner, which needs almost no investment, does this. Such examples include people singing in the local trains, an old man drumming a steel plate at the traffic signal, a child removing his shirt to wipe the windscreens of cars waiting at crossroads and a woman leper playing jingles in the streets. One can also see a blind man playing a mouth organ and collecting money for doing so. The lazy lumps who are as fit as fiddles and refuse to do any work need to draw an inspiration from such people and take such instances as an encouraging example to work.

It is a common sight seeing people stealing a look at

others cards while gambling. We can also see people shouting themselves hoarse on the floor of a stock exchange and signaling about stock prices. It is also a common sight at the racecourse to see people shouting, "Buck up" and calling out the names of their horse who proves to be either a darling or a demon for them. Watching people hunting for the number of their lottery ticket in the list of winners just like students' searching for their roll number is a good experience. If the number of the ticket is present in the list, the spontaneous dance of victory may begin and if the number is absent, sometimes the choicest abuses are spat out in frustration. These are some of the situations in which people want to make a quick buck.

When we travel from one destination to another and look around we can see how different people make money in different ways. We can see a homeless person picking up bricks on his head to make a home for somebody, a hungry man cooking food at a roadside eatery and a bald barber shaving somebody's head. One also gets to see a welder doing his welding, a locksmith playing the game of trial and error with his collection of keys and a carpenter working on that piece of furniture which is an important part of everybody's married life. We can see someone collecting the coins after having performed a monkey's mock marriage. A man can be seen sitting on scaffolding in front of a hoarding holding a picture in one hand and a paintbrush in the other. We can also see six people carefully carrying a billboard on their heads and simultaneously riding their cycles. A loss of balance by one would adversely affect the other five. That is what teamwork is all about. We do sometimes get to see a funeral parlour carrying the dead body of someone who died during the course of doing his work. We can also see a man picking up flowers from a grave, making a bouquet out of them and then selling it at a traffic signal. Really different people take different routes to reach the same destination of money. After our journey is over and we have reached our destination, we have got a glimpse of the journey of money.

In the view of many people, to earn money, one has to necessarily undergo the experience of inconvenience. Such people feel that getting money is akin to placing the hand in the mouth of a Doberman dog if not a Tiger. This signifies what a herculean task such people feel it is to earn money. When we see the hard workers working painstakingly with a smile on their faces and finding the so called inconvenience to be a pleasure, we all feel alike. When we see a man in the scorching heat of the sun postponing his lunch to complete his work of breaking the rocks, ploughing the fields etc. most of us are motivated to work hard. After all, it all depends how we look at things. While for the escapists and unenterprising the excuses are in plenty, for the dedicated and the determined the pending work is in plenty.

In life we do come across people who keep on putting in determined efforts to achieve their objective of earning money. Like horses whose side visions are covered by blinkers, such people only focus on the destination of money, which can get them the goodies of life. Just because the thrust is on money making the integrity is not necessarily always diluted or lost. The scrupulously honest only adopt the honest means, by working hard, being fair in their dealings and perspicaciously envisaging the consequences. It is only by the dint of such attributes that such people make it big. On the other hand, the unscrupulous tell lies, fabricate evidence, swallow others right, use muscle power and falsify figures to make money. No matter whether we adopt the straight, crooked or undulating pathway of making money, God undoubtedly has a hand in our success. The honest sometimes become rich and remain rich until they become a victims of the evil elements. The dishonest do not always become rich. When they become rich, they are encouraged to repeat their gambits to become richer but eventually the consequence is always the same. Such people cannot escape the liability of their misdeeds. Eventually they do meet their nemesis but with staggering intensity. The intensity depends upon the magnitude and nature of the misdeeds done by them.

Moneymaking depends on our views.
Money has always been in the news

CHAPTER Nine

Money and Future

Whenever anybody walks forward he keeps looking ahead of him ignoring his shadow which keeps constant company with him. The shadow always follows him though he can see it only sometimes. Every time he turns back he does not necessarily see his shadow. He can see his shadow in the sun and is unable to see it either in the shade or in the darkness. Whenever he is unable to see his shadow he feels that it is not there. This is surely a fallacy. The shadow surely exists but is concealed by darkness. Similar is the situation in the walk of life where our past travels itself into the future halting itself temporarily in the present. This holds good for all the people who are from the different walks of life. Very seldom due to our deeds of the present the past becomes a page of history, which has been read, flipped away and forgotten. More often than not, our past controls our future making it dance to its tune subject to the limited role of the present.

As each one of us dreams of a bright future we all work to achieve it. To make the future secure one has to administer oneself carefully in the present. Money has always been related to yesterday, today and tomorrow. We must bear in mind that our today is going to become our tomorrow. After that happens we cannot change our yesterday. One has to live in the present and think of the future. The brightness does not come into the future on its own. It has to be worked for.

One has to make several sacrifices in the present for the sake of the future. Different types of sacrifices are to be made at different points of time. Lessons are to be learnt from our past which are to be remembered in the present to plan out the future. The lessons are to be learnt not only from our own experiences but also from the experiences of others around us. The consequence is to be borne in mind before taking the action. As the future cannot be foretold, its uncertainties are to be taken into cognizance while building our futuristic plans.

Money is a key component of a bright future. The future can never be bright without money. Money infuses life into our future. The key factor that is needed to make our future secure is to have an ambition. Ambition is the road that leads us to money. Our ambition must be realistic. It must be possible and practical to fulfil the ambition. Our interests, strengths, weaknesses and constraints must be considered in determining our ambition. For fulfilling our ambition we have to put in the required amount of hard work. To achieve success we must fix different time frames by which different achievements should be made. It could be possible that one is working hard but still not getting the desired results. If failure is experienced, the reasons that are responsible for the failure should be investigated. Thereafter steps should be taken to remove the cause of the failure to achieve success. Sometimes the reason could be that one is working hard but in the wrong direction. Failure must not dishearten us. We must remember that failure is a form of feedback. We must become more determined after experiencing failure. Determination is the key to the door of a bright future. It changes the seemingly impossible into possible. This is one of the many open secrets of making money in the future.

Two brothers, had a widowed mother who had the means of educating them besides giving them a reasonably decent living. She preached her sons to put in earnest effort in educating themselves. She reminded them often that education was the only wealth she could give them. The younger son continuously followed his mother's advice. He shook heaven and earth to make a bright future. He kept his priorities correct and constant. He studied religiously and regularly. In sharp contrast to the younger one, the elder son was not interested in pursuing his studies. He paid no heed to his mother's continous advice. She kept warning him that he was ruining his future but it was in vain. He was busy attending dance parties, making girlfriends, concerned only about his clothes, looks etc. He drew no example from his younger brother. After all, the elder one is not always the wiser one. Time passed by and years kept rolling one after the other. Eventually the younger brother became highly educated and extremely successful. The elder one kept struggling to make his ends meet. Wealth wise, the elder one was junior to the younger one. He kept regretting and repenting about his folly in not educating himself and not listening to his mother. Seeing his younger brother travelling from strength to strength, he felt more and more sorry for himself. It was too late in the day to repent. Time, which had passed away, would never ever return. After all, time is like life, once it is gone it is gone for good. That was the tale of the two brothers. The younger one kept reaping the fruits of his efforts in the past. The elder one became a prisoner of the past.

We do see sometimes that with regard to money matters a widow faces considerable amount of hardship after the demise of her husband. After the death of their husbands, some widows are totally at sea. During the lifetime of their husbands these women had not taken any interest in the financial matters of the family. Moreover their husbands had also not prepared them for such a contingency. Consequently they are unable to either earn or manage money. As such women had earlier led a sheltered life; they land themselves in a sorry and sad state of affairs. There are many unfortunate widows who lose their wealth. This happens either due to their ignorance or their falling a prey to some dishonest people. It would surely be far-sighted and worldly-wise of husbands to teach their wives the recipe of making and managing money. This shall surely be useful in the unfortunate event of the wife becoming a widow. For this the husband must ensure that his wife takes

interest in financial matters. The husband must inform his wife about all their investments, teach her how to manage their investments and how to multiply their money. He should also explain to her what safeguards/ precautions are to be taken on money matters, who are the people she should/ should not rely upon and who are the people she should consult. If the wife is illiterate then the husband should encourage her to get educated. If the husband is a businessman, he must ensure that she starts managing the business under his guidance. He should see that his wife becomes conversant with the intricacies of the business. The husband could consider writing down tips that could be referred to by the wife at the time of need. The husband must question his wife on money matters off and on to ensure that his efforts are not going to be futile. Major children should also be groomed upon on these lines to the extent possible and practical. Such an exercise is bound to be healthy for the future of the family.

In a haste to make more money, some employees leave one job for another. They consider only the size of the salary offered by the new job. The glitter and dazzle of money clouds their judgement completely and they ignore all other vital factors. Such factors are of overriding importance and ignoring these can result in severe damage. These factors comprise of the job profile vis-a-vis their capabilities and experience, permanency of the new job and the work culture at the new place of work. Such factors also include the temperament of the new boss vis-a-vis their tolerance level, market reputation of the employer and the tax liability on the increased income. The future prospects of the new job, the time and means of commuting to and from the place of work and feedback from the employees or ex-employees of the prospective employer are also very important. Sometimes after joining the new employment and earning more, such people realise their folly. Such realisation is followed by repentance. More often than not, their ex-employers refuse to take them back. In a hurry to secure a source of earning more money, they lose their present source of earning money. In trying to reach greener pastures such people reach themselves to unknown pastures which prove to be unsafe. After all it has been rightly said that one must look before one leaps.

Parents must ensure that their children appreciate and acknowledge the importance of money and learn to value it. For this they need to educate their children how difficult it is to earn money. If possible they must take their children to their workplace so that their children realise with what difficulty their parent(s) earn money. Once a while parents must pay cash reward to their children for having made some achievement. This way their children would get the feeling of having earned money. Parents should lay a good example before their children by spending money judiciously. Monetary problems, which can be shared with the children, must be discussed with them. This way their children will start acquiring the attributes that are required to become money managers. By resorting to these practices, parents would definitely do good to the future of their children.

Some children who belong to rich families take the future for granted. The feeling of inheriting in the future destroys their desire to work for a rich future. These children should realise that their family is financially sound today but the fate of tomorrow can never be foretold. History bears testimony that fortunes of many families have nose-dived. Good times can become bad for a variety of reasons. Such reasons include death of the bread earner (which could be followed by subsequent advantages taken by crooked people), fire, floods, earthquake, protracted illness, war, fragmentation of the country etc. It is for this reason that even children of the rich need to concentrate on building their careers for themselves. They should aim at becoming financially independent and self-sufficient. They should remember that there is always a possibility of their parents disinheriting them. After all, the one who owns the wealth enjoys the prerogative of choosing to whom it should be given. Rich parents should not discuss about their riches before their children. They should abstain from discussing about the inheritance by their children in their listening range. However once their children are well settled then they can discuss these matters with them. This would do well to the future of their children.

When one person cheats another by swallowing other's right his future can be guessed. Sometimes even if the culprit buries the hatchet and settles the account with the aggrieved, God does not spare the culprit. Even though due to subsequent soul scratching, a bandit tries to become a just judge, his past deeds follow him like a shadow. Though the victim genuinely forgives the culprit for healing the wounds he has given them, God does not do so. You or I may forgive one another but God will not forgive either of us for our sins. While sending retribution to the culprit, God does not consider the class, caste, creed and colour of the culprit. No amount of money can divert the direction of retribution. It eventually reaches its desired destination. It is for this reason that retribution is said to be divine. Mankind can bribe mankind but mankind can never bribe God. In the greed of making an excellent future, some people land up in a horrible present due to their own irreversible misdeeds of the past.

A dishonest man was really very scared and confused when he saw the police suddenly arriving in his office. The reason being that he was culpable of the offence that brought the police to the office where he was employed. He had stolen a packet containing one hundred notes of denomination of Rupees Five Hundred each. He had distributed these notes to the different pockets of the attire that he was wearing. On seeing the police disembarking from their van and proceeding towards his office, he immediately rushed to the washroom stealthily without making it obvious. As it was a rainy day, a number of raincoats were hung for drying, in the big washroom. Quickly the man emptied all his pockets and filled up the pockets of one raincoat. Before leaving the toilet he ensured that there was not even a single note left in any of his pockets. As he came out of the washroom he conveniently and casually mingled in the crowd. Everybody was searched in person including this man. During the course of the search this man acted most innocently. After all one does not need to be an actor by profession to be good in acting. After the personal search yielded nothing, the proprietor of the firm asked the police to search everybody's belongings, which included their raincoats. Eventually the police unearthed the money from the raincoat, which belonged to the scapegoat. The owner of the raincoat wept bitterly, pleaded innocent but all in vain. The poor victim was not only expelled from his job but also landed up behind the bars. About fifteen years later the scapegoat was requested by a blind man to help him to cross a road. He spoke to the blind man for sometime and then helped him to cross the road. After the road had been crossed, the blind man continued to hold his hand firmly. Much to his surprise, the blind man said that he was his ex-colleague. He confessed that he was the one who had put those notes into his raincoat. Though he had lost his sight, his ears had helped him to recognise his ex-colleague. He had recognised the voice of the person he had wronged. He said that after having lost both his eyes he had become very repentant for the offence he had committed. At times when a culprit begins to suffer, he, in retrospection begins to repent. Moreover one does not need eyes to peep into ones innerself. That was the story of the wrongdoer and the wronged. It was yet another instance of the past pouring itself into the future because of money.

When a relative or friend treats another very shabbily, looking down upon him due to his poverty, the reaction is sometimes surprising, especially so when the (earlier) poor relative or friend becomes much richer than him. If that happens, the high-hander has his hands trembling in repentance. No matter how hard he tries to come close to the rich one, he is more often than not treated indifferently. This is because of the memories of the past which are deeply engraved in the heart of the (now) rich man. When we live in the present we need to remember that a future is sure to follow, which could put us in answerable situations.

We get money in the past, present and future depending upon the effort we put in from time to time. Some people do not put in the required amount of effort and conveniently blame their destiny for not making enough money. Such people fail to remember the old adage- " Man is the maker of his destiny". When we keep putting in dedicated and determined effort, even Nature starts helping us.

CHAPTER Ten

Money and Greed

In their materialistic greed,
many make others bleed.

Some greedy first kill
and subsequently use the will.

The cheated are made to lament
and the greedy have to repent.

Money in any form has always had an age-old relationship with greed. Money has always been playing hide and seek with greed from generation to generation. Greed has always hankered for the friendship of money that has been keeping it at bay. It is a fact that greed has also carried out espionage on money to make it its own. The more greed chases money the further money runs away from greed. Sometimes money obliges greed by making friends with it but such friendship is either short-lived or eventually causes a litany of disasters.

As money is of immense value to all of us, we all desire to possess it. The intensity of this desire varies from person to person. When this desire crosses a reasonable level it gives birth to greed. Those who have such levels of desire for money are greedy for it. The higher the desire for money is from a reasonable level, the greedier is the one who harbours the desire. Those who succumb to greed eventually become its victim. First they see greed as their best friend and then they discover that it is their worst enemy. History bears testimony that greed has never proved to be beneficial to anyone.

There is a very thin line of demarcation, which separates honesty from dishonesty. It is temptation that provokes and prompts people to move from honesty to dishonesty. People who become a victim of temptation eventually cut a sorry figure and eat humble pie. We must careful about temptation. Temptation gives birth to greed, which has ruined several lives.

Some people have this habit of craving to own anything good possessed by somebody else. Without asking for it directly such people adopt all sorts of ways.to extract such goodies. Such ways include over appreciating the eyed article in the hope that it reaches them voluntarily, resorting to circumlocution to send the required message to the owner and even speaking prevaricatingly so that the owner starts desiring to disown the article. The articles yearned for by the greedy elements comprise of cars, coats, fruits, flowers, sarees, suits, watches and also wardrobes. They repeat the same tactic again and again with the same person or with different people. As a result of their own doings but against their wishes they are eventually identified as greedy. It is then that they have to cut a sorry figure. After all greed is too determined to cause embarrassment to its owner.

When two educated sisters who are married to two brothers fight at the time of inheritance of the wealth of their common in-laws, the scene is worth watching. One sister is an advocate and the other is a chemical engineer. In their greed they fight like cats and dogs in public view. The two sisters clench their teeth at one another, snort in reaction, wash one another's dirty linen in public and cite old examples of meanness of the other. One pulls the skeletons of the other out of the cupboard after securely locking up her own skeletons. The elder one raises her hands and the younger one raises her voice and both raise an alarm. As their parents are common and one cannot abuse the parents of the other there is a practical difficulty. This is overcome by filthily abusing the dead in-laws and one another's husbands. Decency demands that I should not reproduce those abuses but it does not prohibit me from leaving these to your imagination and experience. The onlookers form a poor opinion about the two sisters, thanks to their bad behaviour and vocabulary which does not match their educational qualifications. It is surely unbecoming of educated people to behave in such a wild way. The wealth of the dead in laws is finally distributed equally to their satisfaction. Thanks to the husbands who work out a compromise. The wise but not so literate brothers, unlike their wives, do so by resorting to peaceful confabulations. After all one does not have to be educated to be wise. Due to the pandemonium created by the sisters, they earn a bad name. After their spell of anger is over, the two sisters repent for their bad behaviour. Eventually they bury the hatchet. Alas, the damage done by them to their reputation could not be repaired!

In their utter greed for money some people slyly and shamelessly go to the extent of robbing other people's assets. Such assets comprise of different items such as jewellery, flower pots, clothes, stationery and even decorative items from the drawing room. Unfortunately on being caught red handed such people have a lot of explaining to do besides cutting a sorry figure. They are very upset with the fact of having been caught. Salvaging the situation and convincing people with their version of the story is their desperate desire. After a lot of brain storming they help themselves with a doctor's certificate. The dishonest doctor's certificate states that such a person is a kleptomaniac. After all, it is better to be branded as a kleptomaniac than to be branded as a thief. One fine day the truth is told in confidence to a friend who is scrupulously honest and disapproves of such dishonesty. It is then that the thief gets exposed beyond doubt proving conjectures to be true. Someone had rightly said that we couldn't fool all people at all times. Moreover the truth always finds some way or the other to escape out of captivity.

Sometimes one of the elements from a respectable family proves to be the black sheep. This could be due to influence

of his company. The influence of ones company has largely a great impact on ones outlook and even integrity. One such fellow had ruined his outlook, integrity and reputation. Thanks to the wrong type of people he had kept company with right since his impressionable years. His companions had reduced him to a man without any integrity. After all habits inculcated at an impressionable age do have a long lasting impact on us. His success story was the sob story of some sad soul. He arrives at a party. As soon as he arrives all eyes are drawn towards him. The reason is his excellent clothes, shoes and other accessories. Moreover this man is tall, dark and handsome. While he impresses everybody, only his heart knows the true story of his greed with the help of which his outer self looks so attractive. It is surely not wise to judge a person only on the basis of his exterior and ignore his inner attributes. The trousers he is wearing are ill gotten as those were robbed from a relative's place where he had gone to stay. Under the trousers the underwear that he is wearing had been successfully shoplifted from a departmental store. His silk shirt was extorted from a married man who was blackmailed about his infidelity. He wore a watch, which was removed by him from the dead body of his uncle when he had gone to his house at the time of his death. This deplorable deed was done when he was alone in the room with the dead body while others were weeping elsewhere in the house. The expensive pair of shoes he was wearing had the history of having been slyly and unilaterally exchanged for his torn slippers at the footsteps of the temple. Really sometimes people whose external appearance is so good can have such a horrible heart that enables them to commit atrocities without any feeling of guilt. Thanks to their integrity, which is destroyed due to constant company, they keep. After all one must be careful about the company one keeps. More often than not, one's company is bound to cast its shadow on oneself.

In their greed to inherit the old aunt's wealth who lives with them some people stoop so low. Such crooks in the family cajole and coax the old aunt to gift away her wealth to them. The old lady has the horse sense that all the hospitality and good behaviour by the greedy nephews may suddenly stop once she makes the gift. The greedy elements take the thumb impression of the illiterate old lady on a gift deed while she is fast asleep after having taken her daily dose of sleeping pills. The stain of the ink on her thumb is also washed away slowly while she is in her sleep. Within few days of the incident three out of the four nephews who were party to the horrendous sin get killed in a motor car accident. The one and only survivor is flummoxed when he hears of the incident. He dreads of facing the similar consequence or may be even worse consequences. He repents in his solitude and contemplates confessing to the old aunt. The thought of confessing keeps coming into his mind, then going out of it to again come back. The on and off process is like a stroboscope working at a discotheque. Eventually on his own accord he tells his aunty of what he had done along with the other relatives who had died in the accident. Very sheepishly he awaits her response. To his utter astonishment, the aunt reacts saying that she was aware of what happened. The reason being that their ex-maid servant had spilled the beans to her. She says that she has already forgiven all the four people who were accomplices in the act. She says she is still indebted to them for giving her refuge in their house and being so solicitous towards her ever since she started staying with them ten years back. She recalls how the four of them had once saved the life of her late husband. She cites two instances when the four had nursed her wholeheartedly while she was seriously ill. She also remembers how they had assaulted an eve-teaser that had taken liberty on her late daughter. After all, some people do remember the good overlooking the bad. The four had done all these good deeds before they had lost their honesty. She concludes the conversation by saying " God love you as I do." Her nephew tears the gift deed to pieces in her presence. Having done that, he swears to never cast an evil eye on her wealth.

Thereafter he acts a good custodian of her wealth. Her attitude had made her life rewarding. We need to remember that gratitude begets goodness. Moreover when we return good for bad, we could benefit for the good.

A woman asked a male motorist for a lift in his car requesting him to drop her to a particular destination. It was evening time and the motorist was all alone in the car. The motorist stopped the car. The women sat comfortably

in the car and then pulled the door. The car took off and the wicked woman started ogling the gold chain, diamond studded rings and the gold bracelet of the gentleman. The man was indeed a gentleman in the true sense of the word.

After sometime the woman tore her blouse and threatened to accuse the man of attempting to rape her. She hastened to add that if he gave her his gold watch, purse and other valuable accessories, she would cover herself with her shawl and quietly disembark from the car. She also threatened him of the consequences of attempted rape. The poor man's hands were shivering and mind was upset. With all those utterances the women had made the situation volcanic, almost ready to erupt. Being left with no choice he parted with all his valuables and then he stopped the car. The woman used her shawl and got off from the car with the valuables she had stolen. The gentleman deeply regretted giving a lift to the woman. He realised that it is not safe and wise to rely on complete strangers. He also felt that the appearance of the woman whom he presumed to be a respectable lady had carried him away. Three months later he went to an office to realise that the same woman worked there. Fortunately his friend was holding a very senior position there. It is then that the gentleman felt that he could make that woman stand an excellent chance of being expelled from the office. The entire episode was related to his friend who called the woman to his chamber. She had been working in that office for five years but nobody there knew of her greedy and disgraceful deeds. His friend gave her a piece of his mind and told her to return all the things she had extorted from the visitor three months back. Her home was a stones throw away and she was told to get all that stuff from her house after she confessed that it was lying at home. She was also told that she would be pardoned if everything were returned. Within an hour she returned with all those items dear to the victim. The gentleman checked up to find everything to be in order. Thereafter both the gentlemen came out to the open hall with her and unravelled the truth. To that she was given dirty and disapproving looks by all her colleagues especially the ladies. There was a unanimous outcry for her expulsion. The woman lost both her job and her reputation. She had also earned the dubious distinction of being a blackmailer. After all when one threatens somebody of tarnishing his reputation then his own reputation is tarnished. After all in spite of its titanic size the world proves itself to be small at times. Which is why we have to careful and cautious in what we say and how we behave. We never know when, where, how and before whom we become answerable for our utterances and our doings.

A girl from an idealistic family, which is rich in values but not rich in money, gets married. After her arranged marriage she discovers to her dismay that everybody in the joint family is a money monger and each one is playing one up the other for the sake of money. The family comprises of various members with the same attribute of greed with varying magnitude. She finds the house comprising of four other members to be a liar's paradise. As she is observant and analytical, she is careful about the family members whom she knows to be a bunch of liars. Which is why they can cause her no damage. After all, it pays to be observant and analytical. Everyone around her tells lies in their greed, which sometimes sounds like the gospel truth. Though such elements tell lies they make convincing statements. Such statements include " I will become a widow if I am telling a lie." "All my three children will die if I am telling a lie." "I will become crippled if I am telling a lie." " I will become blind if I am telling a lie." At times one of the weird elements utters "If it is proved that I am telling a lie, I will cut off my right hand." He also utters "I will be entangled by an octopus if I am telling a lie." "I will be slapped severely by a monkey if I am telling a lie." The facial expressions, reactions and body language of the liars exposes their lies. After all, liars cannot afford to be poor actors. Moreover lies always have loopholes which are instrumental in exposing it. Furthermore the truth always finds some way or the other to make lies cut a sorry figure. As time passes the girl's greedy sister-in-law leaves the house after her marriage. Thereafter the two brothers of her husband get married to girls who are completely content. The three strong-minded wives transform the three husbands slowly but surely. They do so by repeatedly citing examples of different people who in their greed have met disaster. Thereafter even the only sister of the three brothers is also repeatedly reminded to give up her greed. All the elements that are not greedy anymore find peace after giving up their greed. After all life is more peaceful for the content as compared to the greedy. Moreover, any marriage does some good in some way or the other.

By and large those who dedicate themselves to their work resorting to the honest means and pray for their success are not eventually disappointed. The time, energy, imagination and trouble that people spend to greedily get money should be used for more productive purposes. I hope you will agree with me. Even if you have agreed you would appreciate that this is better said than done. One thing is for certain. If each one of the greedy gives up a little bit of his greed then surely this world would be a better place to live in.

CHAPTER Eleven

Money and Jealousy

Where wisdom is in dearth,
there money gives jealousy birth.

Some are jealous of the rich
and that makes them itch.

Few jealous stoop so low,
that there is nowhere to go.

From time immemorial jealousy has always followed money like a shadow. The money and the jealousy have never belonged to the same person. Some people see others in a privileged position and their heart burns in jealousy. Such people probably feel that by being jealous they too shall find some way of acquiring money. Such people fail to realise that in being jealous they suffer themselves and the moneyed people, whom they envy are unaffected by their jealousy. There is surely an outcome emanating out of jealousy. The outcome is the deterioration or sudden snapping of relations between the moneyed and the jealous or others who are victims of the jealousy. Such a situation is a common consequence that both you and I get to see.

Jealousy is of two types. One type of jealousy is when a

person who is not financially well off is jealous of a moneyed man. The other type of jealousy is when a moneyed man cannot digest somebody else becoming rich. In such situations the rich man feels threatened that if his friend or neighbour or relative also becomes rich, his own importance shall be diluted or lost. This is surely a crooked, selfish and mean line of thinking. In a situation where the poor is jealous of the rich the reason is somewhat understandable. After all every one of us wants to improve one's financial position. Generally the type of jealousy in which a rich man resents another becoming rich is transparent amongst certain type of people. Such type of people are the ones who had been dreaming of becoming rich and eventually their dreams have came true. These people fail to realise that just as they became rich, others too have every right to become so.

Different people adopt different tactics in pouring out their jealousy. Some strange people spread the most barefaced lie in their jealousy. Some people hunt with vulture's eyes to find some flaw or the other in the rich and then make a ceremony of their achievement. Some people in their jealousy quickly quote a foolish statement made by their rich associate. Sometimes those who listen to the foolish quotation either laugh or back chat about their rich associate. Such characters fail to realise that we all make some stupid statement at one time or the other. Some people maliciously bitch about the rich even questioning their character at times. Such custodians of

character are unable to honestly answer questions about their own character. We do get to seeing people staring minutely at the cars, clothes, houses, jewellery etc. of the rich, with their face changing colour rapidly. One also gets to see people having the common characteristic of jealousy flocking together, whispering about the rich and looking at one another in helplessness. Sometimes even from the normal conversation of some people their jealousy is evident. In our lives we get to hear different utterances made by the jealous. Such utterances include " He is extremely rich but equally dangerous. He has this habit of collecting other peoples' skeletons in his cupboard." " He may be rich but he is an outright liar. He carries his loads of lies with him to wherever he goes." " Your cock eyed country cousin may be rich but he is surely rude, shrewd and crude." and " She may be richer than me but then she is surely not even as half as pretty as me." Such utterances also include " Hello rich lady. How is your handsome husband?" " She is extraordinarily good hearted, exceptionally pretty and extremely rich. In spite of all these positive attributes she is undoubtedly uncultured to the core." "By honest means nobody can become so rich. I am sure they must have done some wrong somewhere" and "I cannot understand from where the hell did they make so much of money." By making such utterances the jealous only help themselves to get exposed. Some people turn one person against another in their frustrated feeling of jealousy. The searching questions put forth by some inquisitors confirms their jealousy.

Different people have different ways of letting out their jealousy. A jealous person tries hard to conceal his jealousy but his behaviour always exposes it. When that happens the jealous person is not comfortable and sometimes has to do his share of explaining.

Two families were very friendly with one another for quite sometime. The parents of the husbands had known one another for the last three decades. The husbands had studied together right from their kindergarten days to their post-graduation. Due to this, the husbands were very good

friends. Moreover the two had the same likes and dislikes. The wives also got along very well though that is not necessarily always the case. The two families including their children had been going together for movies, had potlucks in either of their houses, went for picnics together and jointly enjoyed life. The two families had been in association with one another for a good fifteen years and jointly dreamt of becoming wealthy. One fine day one of the families came to know that about a fortnight back the husband of the other family had inherited Rs.50 lakhs from his uncle. The inheritor and his family carefully concealed this information from the other family to preclude them from asking for money. It had leaked out from a blabber-mouthed neighbour of the deceased uncle. The day the family came to know about the inheritance by the other family there was a stony silence in their house. Everybody was quiet in jealousy for quite sometime. Thereafter they felt hurt that their friends did not inform them about the inheritance. The news was brought home by the husband at 6.00 p.m. after he returned from work. The family slept sometime at midnight and skipped their dinner in depression. The reaction had moved from silence to whispers to angry rumblings. The family felt cheated as if the entire amount of Rs. 50 lakhs had been pulled out of their pockets and pushed into the pockets of the other family. Trifle matters relating to difference of opinion and slight selfishness were actively discussed and turned into grudges born out of jealousy. The wife had also finished crying in jealousy and the children had finished wiping her tears. The two families met once again but now the climate had changed. The family of the inheritors were given envious looks and a complete cold shoulder. Their questions were answered in monosyllables. Of course the jealousy was within and the cause of the unwarranted and meaningless grudge was not disclosed. As time passed, the distance between the two families started increasing. The distance was due to the jealous attitude of one family that was well understood by the other. The friendship of decades was eventually reduced to nothingness. As time ticked away, the jealous family started finding fault in their own reaction to the inheritance by their friends. The reason was that a common friend of the two families made the jealous family realise that their grudges were illogical and meaningless. He pointed out the fault lay with them and not with the family of the inheritors. The jealous family started missing their friends. But their friendship had been eaten up by their jealousy. Anything precious possessed by us has to be treasured and nurtured with care. If we fail to do so, we realise the worth of it once we lose it.

Jealousy is a dedicated and determined traitor. It always betrays the one who houses it. Till date nobody has ever benefited by resorting to jealousy. We ought to realise that jealousy eventually causes damage to the jealous. The jealous people do not realise that their jealousy shall never fill up their pockets. The time, imagination, idle gossip, loose talk etc. that is wasted in jealousy should be utilised productively so that the jealous people benefit themselves. If the jealous people resort to such a line of thinking then instead of envying the rich they may become rich themselves.

CHAPTER Twelve
Money and Relationship

More often than not, money has been responsible for the birth, growth, deterioration and even the death of relationships. This is in view of the fact that money itself is related to relationships. This relation probably dates back to the time when money was introduced in the world. In the present day, money needs no introduction to anyone because ever since its birth it has become immortal and of course immemorable. Though men have come and men have gone from the world, money has continued to exist in the world. Quite often we see that money makes relationships dance to its tune controlling their movements. This can be likened to the fingers, which control the puppets dancing at a puppet show. Money has stood the test of time and been responsible for change in human relationships. Such change has caused several consequences such as abortion, birth, enmity, murder, suicide, heartache and war.

It is due to money that people build up relationships such as student and teacher, actor and director, landlord and tenant, master and servant and of course a restaurateur and a gourmet. In the case of blood relations it is not money, which gives birth to relations such as brother, father, mother, sister, uncle etc., but surely it is money which keeps the relationship going. The end of relationships is also a consequence that sometimes owes its credit to money. This is in veiw of the fact that relationships are broken due to the onset of poverty, the theft of money, the usurping of property, the fabrication of figures and of course the swallowing of others monetary right.

When a man becomes rich, by and large people flock around him as if he is distributing unlimited amount of money unconditionally. When the same man becomes poor, the very people who once yearned to be around him flee away from him as if he has contracted an illness that could be contagious for them. These people give this illness the name of paucity of money or poverty and feel it is contagious as he may ask them for money, which would result in a difficult situation. To evade the difficult situation, people maintain their distance feeling that prevention is better than cure. First flanking around the rich man with pride and subsequently keeping him at bay without any apology or guilt is surely shameful on the part of such parasites and

opportunists. Such people crowd around the rich man just like mushrooms suddenly spring up. The more the money he gathers the more is the population of such people and the closer they come to him. On the other hand, when the same man loses his wealth, the very people disappear just the way dancing dolphins duck back into the water. By the same analogy the more the riches the unfortunate one loses, the more is the population of the people who desert him and the further is the distance they keep. When a rich man becomes poor and is shunned away by his fair weather friends, he feels discarded. Whenever I see such a person I am reminded of an abandoned tap with a wash basin thereunder at a railway platform. Of course there are some good souls amongst us who extend their helping hands to pull out such unfortunate ones out of the wilderness. In doing so surely it can be said that one conducts the process of cleansing one's soul. After all even today in this selfish world there are people who make our world a better place to live in.

Some people strongly hold the view that valuable time should not be wasted in building up unadvantageous relationships. They feel that time should be put to productive use by being associated with the rich. Such a view is generally held by opportunists who are not rich themselves. It is a different story that when in the company of the rich, such people temporarily feel rich without actually being so. Such people feel it is a matter of pride to be identified as an associate of the rich. Such parasites think that they shall get a lot of advantage out of their friendship with the rich. One can even overhear such people telling their children "Greet that Aunty respectfully. You don't know how well her house is decorated." "That gentleman is a multimillionaire. You know his son studies in your class. You must make friends with him. Your friendship with him will do you a lot of good." "Today we are not having any lunch. That way we will be able to do justice to the food at the dinner party tonight." When a rich person arrives at the house of such people at that time when somebody who is not rich is being entertained out of compulsion then the scene is worth watching. Question marks are suddenly worn on the face of the host who looks at the visitor who is not rich. This is done to imply that it is time for him to take his walking ticket. After that guest goes the host is too happy to be left alone with the rich man who is served all his favourite items. Free entertainment is also provided to the rich guest by speaking of his favourite topics and even providing laughter at the expense of others. When the rich man leaves the house of such people they have mixed feelings. One side they are happy that they were visited by the rich whilst on the other side they feel as if wealth has walked out of their house. Such parasites keep record of the birthdays and anniversaries of the rich so that such occasions can be exploited to come closer to them. Of course on festivals the rich find place in the list of privileged people to be greeted in priority. If a rich associate of such parasites cheats someone then their reaction can be foretold. They sell their conscience and shamelessly sacrifice the truth. Being fully aware of the full truth, they pretend to be ignorant of it. They are in a tearing hurry to give the benefit of doubt to the rich cheat. As if that was not enough, they even act as the spokesperson of the rich cheat. Thanks to the monetary favours extended by the rich cheat. Whenever such favours are not forthcoming, these parasites expose the rich cheat. Continuously and frantically carrying out a manhunt for the moneyed people is their favourite pastime. Thereafter they preplan their meeting the rich targetted for friendship giving it the colour of meeting by accident. One cannot understand what purpose doing all these gimmicks and resorting to such game plans solves. This is particularly true in view of the fact one does not become rich by being friends with the rich.

Sometimes money brings about a complete radical change in relationships. A person who was all along idolised as a saint and almost worshipped due to his being continuously and carefully respected by us, is instantly insulted on being seen by us. After having been treated like a saint, the same person is subsequently treated like shit. Much to his horror such a person has to see hatred writ large on the faces of those who once loved him intensely. This is due to the contribution made by him, which results in a disaster of emotions. Such a contribution is due to a breach of trust committed by him in money matters. When we entrust somebody with money, there is always a possibility. Such a possibility is the turmoil he has with his conscience due to the diluting of his integrity. The dilution process is either on his own accord or attributable to his spouse, children, relatives, friends etc. Initially the integrity goes up to come down and again go up just like the waves in the sea or an ocean. The singsong process carries on and then eventually greed grabs away the better of him. This results in continuous confrontations between the two parties who even exchange explosive words. Regular fights take place due to the trusted turning himself from a bosom friend of honesty to a bosom friend of dishonesty. Such consequences result in the off take of animosity between the two people. Examples of these sort of situations include a sister proving herself to be a sinisterer, a brother proving himself to be a Brutus, a best friend proving himself to be a worst enemy and so on and so forth. Sometimes the aggrieved becomes like a volcano of hatred erupting its lava. The lava in such cases comprises of arguing with acid tongued fury and cursing intensely including the burning desire that the betrayer dies a dog's death. This is all due to the tryst of money with temptation, which could result in betrayal. After all money has both its givings and misgivings.

Turbulent times teach all

of us a lesson that we need to learn. It is our period of struggle that helps us to distinguish our fair weather friends from our good companions. It does happen in the world that we get to see a rich man becoming poor. When this happens the poor person is more often than not devastated, as he has to experience not only the curse of poverty, but also the insincerity of his supposedly sincere friends and relatives. In those days when this person was rich, he kept lavishly loading his friends with presents, entertaining them at reputed restaurants and hosting glittering parties. Unfortunately most of the people who had accepted his hospitality conveniently forget it, start distancing themselves from him and get busy disowning him. Such people behave alike but make different utterances. Such utterances include "Why do you come here?" "In future please do not come here." "I do not wish to take his call. Tell him I am not available." "Whom are you talking about? I don't know him." "Now you can go." Some see him at a marriage and look the other way. Some see him coming and quickly change their path. Such a consequence is a common feature and has always found its place in the pages of history. It is the good luck of the poor person who meets his old friend who is a rich man. In the good old days when he was rich and this friend was poor it was he who was instrumental in making his friend rich. He had extended money and used his contacts in the past to change the fortune of his friend. When the poor man meets his old friend who is rich he is more than prepared for a cold shoulder but contrary to his expectation he is met warmly. He feels that the old friend is probably unaware of the downswing in his wealth level. He is surprised and pleased to learn the old friend knows everything and holds deep gratitude towards him. His friend says "I was always your friend and I was never the friend of your money." Travelling to nostalgia, his friend says "You were the one who threw light on my dark days. I have remembered you and your good at every stage of my life." After all, gratitude is still alive in this largely crooked world. History repeats itself and now the poor man is rehabilitated and pulled out of the lurch by the help, contacts, guidance and money of his old friend. His friend responds to his thanksgiving by saying, "Friends do not need a Thank You." Time climbs from days to months to years. Eventually he is once again rich. Now he is much richer than what he was earlier. Though he becomes rich once again his outlook is different now. He is now careful and wise to distinguish between the hypocrites and the sincere. That is what the ups and downs of life do to people.

CHAPTER Thirteen
How to Save Money

Comparative Study: If we survey the market before we incur our expenditure, we would undoubtedly save our money. This is because sometimes the same product or service is available at a lower price. In such situations, the service or product, which is costlier, provides no additional advantage. Sometimes even if such an advantage is provided, it is of no use to us. Amongst other situations this holds good for consumer products, package holidays, cost of air tickets to travel abroad etc.

Avoid impulsive buying: We should avoid window-shopping. Sometimes while doing window-shopping people end up making purchases. Such purchases should be made wisely and not impulsively. On such occasions we need to tackle our temptation wisely and should not succumb to it. Things that are purchased impulsively are rarely used.

Credit Card: Some people keep using their credit card recklessly and foolishly. They realise their mistake only when they receive their credit card bill. Such people land up in debt and call their credit card the culprit. The fact remains that they should blame themselves and not their credit card. We should carry our credit card with us but with it we must not carry the habit of using it irrationally.

Communication Costs: The mode of communication chosen must be decided on the basis of the urgency of the message. If the message is not urgent it can be communicated by ordinary post. If the matter is urgent, one can choose between E-Mail and telephone. Outstation calls should be short and should be preferably made when the rates are low. If the addressee has an E-Mail address but does not open the mail regularly then this mode should not be used. If such a mode is used, as the message is long and urgent then the addressee must be told over phone to open the mail.

Patience Pays: With the advancement of technology and cutthroat competition amongst manufacturers, it is the consumer who stands to benefit. In certain areas, the longer a consumer postpones an expenditure the more is the possibility of the same product / facility being sold/ available at a lower cost. Sometimes if one follows the decreasing trend of prices in the market, one is likely to benefit. If the grapevine talk says that the Government's budget, which is in the offing, is likely to reduce the price of certain products, it may be worth waiting.

Cost of Electricity: At times when we visit the house of someone we see that a particular room is unoccupied and unattended. It is unattended as nobody has paid any attention to the wasteful or avoidable expenditure that is being incurred in that room. This is because lights, fans, television etc. are left switched on in the room. Such wasteful expenditure should be avoided. In places where an air cooler can be used, people should think before using their air conditioners. Instead of always using their air conditioner people should also use their air cooler depending on the weather.

Saving Taxes: Many people pay taxes that can be legally and legitimately avoided. This is due to their ignorance of the tax laws. If we fulfill certain conditions spelt out in the tax statute then we are entitled to enjoy a lower liability of tax. One such condition is making specified investments within the stipulated time. We need to remember that tax planning results in tax reduction.

Size of the house: The number of the members in the family, the frequency of visits by outstation guests, the number of married couples in the family, separate space for children to study etc. should determine the size of the house in which one lives. Sometimes we see a family of two members ignorantly living in a house having six rooms. One must remember that the size of a rented house determines the size of a regular expenditure. The size of a house owned by someone determines the amount invested and the interest/income forgone.

Preserve Discount Coupons: Sometimes some companies give us discount coupons, which can be availed of while buying their products. These are generally given to those people who hold either shares or fixed deposits in the company. At the time of receiving these coupons we think that we would not be using them. Subsequently when we wish to use such coupons, these are not traceable. We would benefit if we preserve such coupons and remember their expiry date.

Reduce eating out: One must control the frequency of dining out. Eating out is an expensive affair. If one is eating out very often, the frequency must be reduced. Instead of eating the entire meal out it may be worthwhile to cook the food at home and call for an exotic dish from an outside eatery. When one eats one must be careful in the quantity one orders. The quantity of food must ordered thoughtfully and not impulsively. Quite often at restaurants we see people leaving food as the quantity ordered was in excess of that required.

Middleman's Commission: More often than not, direct dealing between the buyer and the seller reduces the cost for the buyer. This is because engaging a middleman involves a cost component which automatically gets eliminated in direct (Broker's excuse) transactions.

Avail of off-season discount: We surely stand to benefit if we make purchases in the off season. It pays to buy our woolens in the summer and our air conditioner in the winters.

Exchange Offers: These schemes offer us more value for money. By opting for these schemes we can exchange our old assets such as refrigerator, air conditioner, electric iron etc for new ones.

Wholesale Markets: Many people are unaware that these markets also cater to the retail consumer at wholesale prices. We should consider shopping at these markets. Some such markets are located at far off places. When we intend to visit these areas primarily for some other work, we could also plan to shop at such markets.

Economy Packs: It is economical to buy certain products in larger quantities. Larger quantities of some products prove to be cheaper than smaller quantities. Probably this is why larger packs are called economy packs. We need to bear this in mind whenever we go shopping.

Check out time: This is important when we stay at a hotel. If we check out the check out time before we check in, we could save the room rent for a day. We need to bear in mind the check out time whenever we check in or check out of a hotel.

CHAPTER Fourteen
Stinginess

Adopting all available means, some people try to reduce their cost of living. This is surely a constructive exercise as it gives them more value for money. By resorting to such a course of action they get more utility for the same amount of money. We all try to resort to cost cutting exercises at some time or the other and in some way or the other. The million-dollar question is to what extent we should carry out such exercises. The benchmark is different for different people as they all live in different situations. The key reason why their situation is different from one another is the amount of disposable income available to them. However if anybody is over-enthusiastic about his cost cutting exercise, people classify him as stingy. This undermines his image. Sometimes such people make a laughing stock of themselves. It is for this reason that we need to resort to cost cutting judiciously. Our reasoning power should be used to determine the extent, nature and timing of cost cutting.

There are several factors that determine the inclination or otherwise of people to spend money. Such factors include social standing, responsibilities, liabilities, wealth, upbringing, outlook, income and priorities of the people.

It is not easy to find out the reason why one is stingy. However it is easy to brand someone as stingy. Which is why we must refrain from calling someone stingy. But sometimes we are constrained to call some people stingy. The reason lies in their abnormal behaviour, which prompts us to do so.

Many people resort to different cost cutting exercises but do not simultaneously try to increase their income. The cost cutting process is resorted to and the possibility and probability of increasing the income is not visited. Such a course of action is surely not correct. Besides trying to reduce one's cost of living one should also concentrate on increasing one's income. If people adopt this strategy, they would surely be a happier lot.

A couple spent its entire married life most magnanimously distributing its stinginess to the world. They found absolutely no flaw in doing so as the parents of both the husband and those of the wife were masters at stinginess. Born out of such parents, stinginess ran in the blood of both of them due to which their married life was harmonious and happy. Though the couple had a telephone at home, they kept making phone calls from the neighbour's place on the pretext that their phone was out of order. The lie was however never believed. If the husband's friend rung up in his absence requesting the wife to tell her husband to return the call, there was always a standard reply to the effect that there was something wrong with the phone disabling them from making telephone calls. The caller was invariably asked to call back at a fixed time when the husband would be at home. It would be anybody's guess that the husband too followed the same practice. Birthday and anniversary parties were always attended without any present giving the excuse that it was left at home in a haste to reach the party in time. This was also proved by the fact that the couple was first to arrive at the party. Moreover the husband spoke of the wife's penchant for punctuality and the wife spoke of his. That was all a facade in their act of saving the cost of the present. They always said that they would send the present, but it was never sent. Whenever food was served at the party, one ate like a dog and the other like a pig. The talkative couple never uttered a word while they ate the free food. After having eaten to their hearts content, the couple blessed the host for having invited them to the party which they found to be a parasite's paradise. Whenever the stingy couple

received presents, the mouth of the gift horse was opened wide and the couple stared into it. The cost cutting couple would go ga ga if they found the present to be expensive. If the present was an inexpensive one, then the forefathers of the person who gave it were cursed. The lower the cost of the present, the higher was the intensity of the curses. A refrigerator, which was not in working condition, was used most productively, in their bedroom as a cupboard to exploit its storage space. This was done to cut the cost involved in buying a cupboard. Whenever an outstation relative had to be invited for a meal, the scene in the kitchen was never different. Old stale food was used up by purposely cooking the same dishes so that the mixing process would be facilitated. It goes without saying that the quantity was always heavily economised. Junk mail was searched with great enthusiasm to remove and then preserve all those paper clips. Both the husband and the wife kept helping one another in giving the society a topic for discussion.

Sometimes one comes across people who heavily focus on saving money. Such people strongly feel that a penny saved is a penny earned. They live throughout their lives in stinginess and even die in it. They cut different types of expenditures in different ways at different times, hoping to be comfortable at all times. Such people curb their desires and give up good food, good clothes and a good living in the hope of saving up for a good future. As nobody has ever known the future that has always kept everyone guessing, they are sometimes disenchanted. This is illustrative of a situation when in their stinginess they do not take up a medical insurance policy as its premium costs money. The cost of this act committed in stinginess is sometimes too heavy. Such people land themselves in a situation when substantial portion of their savings is spent on medical treatment of unexpected ailments. After all it has been rightly said that too much of anything is bad which surely includes stinginess.

Quite often we come across people with a poor background who have become rich. These are the people whose mentality does not generally change. This variety of people live in tastefully decorated homes but their attitude is tasteless and terrible when it comes to spending money. Such people increase their rent by an insignificant amount when their landlord leaves the quantum of the increase to their generosity. They increase their rent of Rs 500 for the first time in ten years by a ridiculously low amount of Rs 10. They lack the foresight to see the ramifications the low amount of the increase can cause the tenancy arrangement. Angered by the insulting increase, their landlord forces them to vacate the premises. This is their punishment for being so stingy. While making purchases at the vegetable market these people resort to illogical and irrational bargaining. They sometimes have more than one car but petrol is filled into their cars very calculatively. Their visitors are served snacks in their saucers. Such people feel that by being stingy they are being wise. They fail to realise that in the process they are earning a bad name.

At the crossroads one can see people taking change from a beggar. Some find nothing wrong in doing so while others call such an act disgraceful. It really shocks anyone when on the pretext of putting money into a blind man's begging bowl, people take away coins of a bigger denomination than that what they put into the bowl. Some flagrant people say they have dropped in a Note, which makes no sound, and remove coins, which give the blind man a noise to listen. This is what one can call the conversion of utmost stinginess into dishonesty due to the temptation of money.

It is a myth that all rich people are large hearted. Some people are rich because they are small hearted. Such people feel that by economising on their cost of living they can get richer and remain richer for longer. I don't think I would be fully wrong if I say that people with small pockets are the ones with big hearts.

Money is something people do not easily lend.
Money is what some do not easily spend.

CHAPTER Fifteen
Flaunting Money

Some people show off their spending propensity,
without having enough monetary density.

Too often if people show off their purse,
then they may get the jealous curse.

When the upstarts begin to flaunt,
others find reason to taunt.

The aforementioned gives anybody an aerial view of how people exhibit their money and what happens when they do so. Seeing people flaunting their money is a common sight. Money is shown off to probably gain recognition and respect in the society. Many of us think that such a view is surely correct. If people were respected only because of their money then the rich gangsters, murderers, tricksters etc. would have been worshipped. It is a different matter that the rich and successful are hero-worshipped by those who are struggling to become rich and successful. Money is just one of the many reasons why people are respected. The qualities and deeds of a person should be the basis of people for being respected or disrespected. People respect us in the short run because of money but in the long run factors other than money decide whether we should be respected or not. Of course some materialistic people take such a decision only on the basis of money. At times their experiences in life teach them what should be the criteria to respect people.

Even at public places of worship some people show off their money. At such places we can see some peculiar people behaving in an absurd manner. They attend the place of worship in their fineries. These are displayed to impress others who have come to say their prayers. They do not realise that a place of worship is not the venue for exhibiting wealth. Such people need to have a dress sense vis-à-vis the occasion. When they have to make an offering, they arrogantly take out their wallets, count the currency notes and make the offering. Such offering is made with the intention of showing off their money to the people around them. A place of worship is the House of God and should never ever be used as a platform to exhibit wealth. Moreover the size of the offering is never important for the Lord. It is the spirit with which one is making the offering that is important.

There are some people who become rich due to the sweat of their brow. After living through a period of struggle they reach a period of success. Some such people keep showing off their money and keep hiding their humble past. They impress others with their money and willfully conceal their past. They feel uncomfortable and embarrassed if the humbleness in their past comes to the fore. It is their view that the good impression created by their present wealth would be adversely affected because of their past. This is surely an irrational line of thinking chosen by their vanity. On the contrary, they must take pride in the fact that they have risen considerably in the ladder of success due to their hard work. Their past testifies their achievements, which have reached them to the present. If such people look at their past from this viewpoint they would be proud of it instead of being ashamed of it.

Some people have this habit of boasting about their parent's wealth. They keep showing off their parent's wealth and take immense pride in doing so. This habit is largely seen in teenagers and even in some adults. Instead of showing off the feathers in their father's/ mother's cap such people show try to collect feathers for their own caps. Such elements fail to realise that nobody appreciates them for the achievements made by their parents. People respect and appreciate us for the achievements made by us and not for those made by our parents.

We do see people resorting to a vulgar display of their wealth while performing the marriage of their children. This is probably done to gain recognition in the society. At times some people keep sacrificing throughout their lives to ensure that they have sufficient money to perform an impressive marriages of their children. Some people even borrow money to perform such marriages. They spend money, which is well beyond than their means. After the marriage is performed they keep suffering because of their folly. Thanks to the requirements of the society that require people to perform an ostentatious marriage. It is difficult to ignore such requirements of the society. However we should attach due and not undue and unnecessary importance to the same. In life we do have to regulate our lives for the sake of others. However we must know where to draw the line. If we follow such a disciplined line of thinking, we would be a happier lot.

Some people reach the destination of money by resorting to dubious means. At times such people make it big. Some

such people flaunt their money for supposedly gaining respect in society. They constantly and continuously boast and brag about their money. Continuously flaunting their money they invite the curiousity of others. After all, people do start taking interest in a person once he/she becomes rich. In their curiosity people try to reason out the source that has made that person so rich. It is then that regulatory and investigative bodies start probing into the quarters from where the riches have been gathered. When the cat comes out of the bag, such people regret and repent for foolishly flaunting their money. They are then caught in their own web and land up in a Catch 22 situation. Having flaunted their wealth vigorously it becomes difficult for them to disown it. This is one of the many misgivings of flaunting money.

By and large it is the fairer sex that takes delight in flaunting money. Besides taking delight in doing so, they also get a meaningless sense of satisfaction in showing off their money. When women who have the common attribute of showing off their money meet, it is really a wonderful scene worth watching. Each one is in a desperate hurry to speak either of her wealth or of the purchase of items by her. Without waiting for the speaker to complete, the impatient listeners are in a rat race to start talking. Obviously the intention of each one is the same but probably the manner of description and the confidence with which the exaggeration is done is different. The ranting is done about the purchase of diamonds, gold, silver, sarees, solitares etc. Besides this the visits to various prestigious places, foreign trips, increasing income of the husband etc. also feature in the conversation. During the course of conversation some women emphatically utter words which are important to them. These words are dropped in the conversation just like eggs are dropped to form the egg drop in a soup that is being cooked. While uttering these words the voice is vibrated and raised to ensure that the listeners cannot miss hearing those wonderful words. Such words include "Five Star", "World Tour", "Crocodile Leather", "Platinum" and of course false figures representing expenditure incurred. Obviously the figures are inflated because they feel the higher the figure, the higher the impression created.

It shall certainly be unfair to accuse only the women folk for flaunting their wealth. Sometimes humble husbands who become rich are brainwashed again and again by their wives to resort to exhibiting their wealth and bragging about their riches. Sometimes such husbands obey their wives and sometimes they defy and reprimand their wives for such peculiar practices. Of course it all depends on the personality of the husband or the wife. Without any influence of the wife sometimes the husband is inherently a money- flaunter even before his marriage, thanks to the ideas drilled into his brain by his parents. At times the showing off is picked up by either of the spouses due to the influence of their nouveau riche friends.

One woman showed off ten items to her visitor who appreciated them encouraging her to show off more and more. The woman kept on showing off her snob value items one after the other. She had flaunted ten items. After the visitor left nine items could be traced but an expensive diamond ring worth Rs 3 lacs was not traceable. The visitor was accused behind his back of secretly doing away with it. The woman made an issue of the financial status of the visitor for justifying her suspicion. The world has a few foolish rich people who feel that those who are not rich are dishonest. There was utter confusion in the house and the combing operation began in full swing. The woman was on the verge of leaving for the visitor's house after she was unable to find the ring in spite of her three-hour search which included bouts of crying. Just then her husband suddenly declared that he had just found the ring in the gap between the sofa and the carpet. The small ring had caused big trouble. The reason was the diamonds studded in it, which had shot up its value and caused the tension. The woman did not proceed for the visitor's home and realised the inherent risk of showing off her money and her stupidity in suspecting the innocent visitor. The maid who was working in the house of this lady had seen her exhibiting her jewellery to the guest. She had also overheard that that diamond ring was worth Rs 3 lacs. Moreover the commotion caused by the lost ring which was finally found had left an impact in the memory of the maid. Thereafter the maid started having sleepless nights due to the jewellery possessed by her mistress. Within a fortnight of this incident the maid came to her employer's house with two of her uncles. The three visited the couple's home when the husband had gone to office. The three looted the jewellery from the lady's house and murdered her. The murder was gruesome. The three had tied up the hands and legs of the lady. They had also stuck cello tape on her eyes, ears and mouth. Then they had strangled her. The murder was committed to ensure that subsequently they would not be identified and exposed. After all, showing off can at times even cost us our lives. Some showoffs unintentionally invite the attention of evil elements. This puts them in a vulnerable situation and their safety is threatened.

When a girl from an inherently rich family marries a boy from a nouvea riche family, there is friction in the ideology of the two. As the girl's family has been rich right from the beginning she can see no reason or logic for flaunting money. On the other hand the boy's parents having become rich after a long struggle, he likes to flaunt his money. The result is that the proud husband tells the wife also to flaunt their money. The wife argues repeatedly questioning the purpose of doing so. When the wife tells the husband that because of their habit of flaunting their money, people laugh at him, his parents, his brothers and sister, he gets skeptical. As time passes, the wife ensures that the same is proved to the husband on several occasions. She does so by seeing to it that her husband listens to the back chatting about his father's family and their showing off. Amongst other utterances he overhears "While this character consciously shows off his money, he fails to realise that simultaneously though subconsciously he keeps showing off his humble past." "His voice gets almost choked with excitement when he races through the experiences he had after he became rich." " In his excitement of having become rich this fellow performs the monkey's dance. He dances with joy while showing off his valuables, which have been purchased, with his new money. He does not realise that he is making a fool of himself." "He describes the taste of expensive dry fruits. At last, this upstart has got money to eat dry fruits." It is then that sense starts setting into the mind of the husband who ceases to flaunt his money. After all, if wives want they can change their husbands for the better.

Though all round us we see people flaunting money but we see no merit in their doing so. Except for resulting in envy by jealous people and flattery by parasites, there seems to be no potent possibility of any productive consequence. This is a situation of their own making. These are hard core truths that the show offs have not realised from generation to generation. Probably most of them shall never realise it till doomsday. One should focus on being financially sound from within as against just being rich in the opinion of others.

CHAPTER Sixteen

Money and Pride

Some rich are proud
and purposely speak aloud.

Few upstarts feel so big,
treating others like a pig.

Either the proud eat humble pie
or in their pride they die.

Pride has sometimes been a consequence pouring itself out of money. Pride need not necessarily be because of money. Different people are proud for different reasons such as good looks, good physique, good figure, good talent etc. To my mind all these good attributes such as looks, physique, figure, talent etc. are just transitional and never last. All the goodness in the looks, physique, figure, talent etc. eventually gets washed away with time.

Money is by no means an exception to this reality and because it has the hallmark of changing hands, its permanency is always vulnerable. In spite of this we get to see so much of pride due to money in the world that it is really surprising. Something that cannot be carried by us when we die should at no cost be the cause for pride.

Knowing that death is inevitable and all the money is going to be left behind here itself people still resort to pride. Whether money or any other reason can never ever be a justification to be proud. The reason being that the existence of pride itself is questionable.

After some people become rich, sometimes they continue to keep company with their old associates who are not rich. More often than not, these associates keep appreciating the laurels of money that have been won by such people. Time and again they keep showering compliments on their rich associate. Such compliments relate to the clothes, car, house and the lifestyle of their rich associate. This starts making such rich people conscious of their riches. Having received compliments regularly, they start shooting self-congratulatory statements. It is then that they take to pride. After they become proud, they sometimes sever their connections with the very people who had pushed them to pride. Is that not really ironical ?

There are various ways in which people show their pride of money. Some proud people abruptly slam down the telephone without bothering to reply to an adieu thereby ignoring the basics of telephone manners. In their pride some people stop using the word "Hello" whenever they answer the phone but utter "Yes". After becoming rich pride can be seen in the gait of some people. In spite of being short, some people who are proud of their money look down at everyone while they are conversing with anyone including the tall. Some people who are proud of their money put a tight facial expression thinking others shall envy them knowing them to be rich. Sometimes without even meeting a rich person one can know of the pride due to the tone of his talking over the telephone. In the pride of their money some upstarts reduce their tolerance level. Their temper is always on a razor's edge. One has to only utter a statement they do not like and they react sharply. Imperiously some people do not permit others to speak because of their pride of being rich. In their pride some people make different statements. Such statements include " I have become too rich to become poor again." " The door of my house should open into a small room which leads to a big drawing room. Being an architect you may know that such a room is called an anteroom. This small room will be useful to drive off all my old acquaintances that come to ask for money. The others will be allowed ingress into the drawing room. Please make the plan of my house accordingly." Such people who are proud of their money look down upon others and treat them high-handedly. When ignorantly and out of habit they behave in such a manner with somebody who is ten times richer than they are, do then the consequence can be foretold. The consequence is that just like they have been treating others shabbily they are treated similarly and snubbed suddenly. This sometimes makes them realise where the shoe pinches. After all no man is supreme in terms of money. There is always someone richer than someone else.

Some people who belong to lower middle class families

suffer from an inferiority complex. They have such a complex as they attach immense importance to being rich and they know that they are far from rich. They cover up such an inferiority complex by putting up a façade of a superiority complex. Without explicitly stating that they are rich they imply in their behaviour that they are rich. Due to their conflicting complexes they sometimes have friction with people. On such occasions they are sometimes snubbed for their false pride and put in their place. It is then that they are rudely reminded about their true position. Paucity of money can also result in pride, which brings about undesirable results. This is a paradoxical position created by money.

Some people have the habit of dealing with others in a proud manner. Just because they have become rich such people feel that the world is under their feet. They are unfair in their dealings as they feel that they can never be wrong. Out of habit they behave in a clumsy manner when they are speaking to others or are being spoken to or are aware of the fact that they are being watched. This behaviour is resorted to due to their misconception that people will be convinced by their motivated mannerisms that they are rich. Having suddenly risen to richness and then observing the behaviour of other upstarts, they are motivated to follow suit. One such woman was moving about the railway platform waiting for her outstation guests to arrive. The train was late by about two hours. The foolish woman in talking to different strangers off and on spent this time. As the delay in the arrival of the train started getting extended the snooty woman found it convenient to check up the arrival details from such strangers. With a proud facial expression her big eyeballs kept moving about to take stock of who was watching her. She kept blinking her eyes just like the eyes of an aeroplane flying in the dark. Though she was extremely fat, she had tied her saree really tight. She wore a frown on her face as she had got irritated having waited for so long. The dazzling diamonds in her ears drew the attention of everyone around her. Thanks to her dark complexion, which highlighted the diamonds and hid the frown. After all a dark complexion provides both an advantage and a disadvantage. Even while talking to the porters pride was shown to them. Bystanders found her to be proud but nobody knew why she was proud. But she knew that she was proud because of her money. She flipped through the photographs in about ten magazines with her fingers, which were bejewelled with diamond rings. She eventually bought a magazine of Rs 10. She handed over a Five Hundred Rupee note to the bookseller. He replied that he did not have any change. She kept the magazine and imperiously ordered him to get the change. He said he would not go to get the change. After all he was not her servant to take her orders. Some rich people have this wretched habit of bossing over the poor including those who are not employed by them. She reacted to that by slamming the magazine on his books and walking away. The train eventually arrived bringing the relatives who were given proud looks and a cold shoulder by her as they were not financially well off. One of the relatives was about to embrace the lady. On seeing that, she moved back and gave the relative a hard stare. The luggage was handed over to a porter who had only one eye. His other eye had been taken away by a vulture. The money was not discussed with the porter. He carried it to her flamboyant car. Then a paltry sum of five Rupees was slammed highhandedly in the hand of the porter for carrying six baggages on his head and over his shoulders. The porter had even travelled the long flight of steps while carrying the luggage. He had done all this hard work though he possessed only one eye. The porter was angry with the raw deal and he voiced his anger. The woman loudly and rudely told the porter to keep quiet. The rich woman started her car and the porter threw the five rupee note into the car and spoke in revenge and frustration of the woman's stupid mannerisms. He even condemned her for being so tiny hearted though she advertised her money in her behaviour. The coxcomb was forced to switch off the ignition of the car as other porters including those who had watched her behaviour during the waiting period fought for the cause of their friend. There was a well-deserved shower of insults, ridiculing remarks and angry rumblings for the stupid woman. After all people either respect or disrespect us depending on the fairness or otherwise of our dealings. In her pride the woman threatened the porter that if he did not keep the note he would get nothing. My God, what amazing arrogance? The porter responded to that by saying that she could keep the pittance as charity. The outstation guests who had been victims of her snobbery on several occasions were extremely happy in their hearts. After having eaten enough humble pie, she drove off leaving the poor porter unpaid. The poor porter watched the car moving away from him. The woman was driving the car and her relatives were travelling in it. The car was carrying the relative's luggage and the woman was carrying the porter's worst wishes. The car started becoming smaller and smaller to the porter's eye and eventually it shrank into invisibility. The unpaid porter felt cheated and had to skip his lunch. Thanks to the rich woman. After all, some people who are so conceited and proud of their money should be ashamed of their deeds.

Six men were very good friends. One fine day one of them won a lottery of Rs 3 Crores. After that happened he fell a victim to pride and drifted away from his five friends. He had been poor for decades and his five friends were still poor. These friends were discouraged to meet him. If they came to his house they were made to wait for an unusually

long time. Then they were questioned of the purpose of their visit and given a cold shoulder. They were not even asked to sit down to encourage them to leave. If they spoke to him then he gave them the shortest possible answer. He travelled in his chauffeur driven flamboyant car seeing them in queue for the bus and looked through them. If he met them by accident he refused to acknowledge their presence. One night when he was travelling in his car with his wife the car suddenly stopped on its own. The husband opened the bonnet but was unable to find out the cause. Both the husband and wife shut the bonnet and locked up the car. They sought a lift from a passing car. The car stopped and three young boys who were under the influence of alcohol misbehaved with his wife. They beat up the husband brutally. The man fell down unconscious. The boys tried to rape the poor woman. At that time hearing the screams of the lady, five men returning from a night show ran to her rescue. The men beat up the boys severely. A police-van, which is on patrolling rounds, passed by. The men stopped the van and handed over the boys to the police. One of the five men removed his shawl and gave it to the lady to cover her torn blouse. Meantime the husband recovered from his unconsciousness. He checked up from his wife about her state. She mentioned about the good deed done by the five men. The man proceeded to thank the five men. They saw his face and tried to make themselves scarce. The reason being that all these five men were the husband's poor ex-friends who had tasted enough of his pride. Two out of these five had in the past requested the husband for a small favour. He could have easily extended the favour by just making a telephone call. As he had wanted to hold them at bay, he had not extended that favour. The man's conscience fought with his pride. Eventually his conscience emerged as the winner. He saw his God in these five men. After all, in life we sometimes discover the Lord in ourselves and sometimes in others. With folded hands and tears rolling down his cheeks the husband thanked these men and apologized for his past proud behaviour. The five men embraced their friend and they too had moist eyes. The six men once again became friends. The bonds of friendship were even stronger than before. Now even pride could do no harm to their friendship. After all, it has not been said for nothing that eventually pride has to have its fall.

CHAPTER Seventeen
Money and Honesty

Honesty is a jewel that cannot be seen but can be felt and experienced. It is that invisible jewel which can be possessed by the rich and the poor, the male and the female, the young and the old, the able and the disabled and of course the black and the white. The jewel of honesty brings striking sparkles in the reputations of people and sometimes makes them immortal in our memory.

In environments where dishonesty looms large it is exceedingly difficult for the honest to retain their honesty. They either sacrifice or sell their credibility or character at the behest of the dishonest. The longer they take to do so, the longer they are made to suffer. Notwithstanding the evil environment some scrupulously honest people refuse to budge an inch from their honesty. Resultantly, whether knowingly or unknowingly, they obstruct the moneymaking methods of the dishonest. Which is why they are harassed, humiliated and even hated by the dishonest. At times the dishonest put in honest efforts to dislodge the honest so that they can promote their dishonesty. These efforts include resorting to various gambits and game plans. If their efforts prove to be futile, they curse the honest for their honesty. The dishonest feel victorious if such efforts bear fruit. Such a victory is always a hollow victory. This is because eventually it is the honest who always have the last laugh.

It is the attitude of people, which speaks of the presence of either honesty or dishonesty in them. When we interact with someone, we get an opportunity of knowing how honest or dishonest such a person happens to be. In this connection, sometimes we get misled in the short run but then in the long run the true colours of the person in question come to the fore. After all in life sometimes we feel that we know a person quite well but later on we realise how badly and sadly we were mistaken.

A lady left the bank after having taken her jewellery from the bank locker. She waved her hand to signal to a passing taxi. The taxi stopped and the lady looked at the bearded driver. The driver had a frown on his face. He wore the frown due to the scorching heat of the sun in which he had been driving in the jam-packed streets for the last five hours. The lady felt that the driver did not seem to be of good intention. She felt so as she had misread his facial expression and his muscular appearance had scared her. Moreover in terms of honesty the driver did not appeal to her at first sight. She presumed that carrying the jewellery in this taxi would be vulnerable. She was contemplating of not travelling in this taxi. As getting another taxi would be difficult she chose to travel in it. She got into the taxi and pulled the door. The driver put the meter down and the taxi took off. While driving, the driver lit a cigarette and began to smoke. This made the lady uncomfortable and she felt that she should not have travelled in that taxi. After all in life some people do doubt the character of those who smoke and drink. The taxi took a turn to avoid the traffic snarl and the suspicious lady's heart skipped a beat. Just as the road was isolated the lady too felt isolated. She was dying for the journey to come to an end. The lady reached her home and quickly disembarked from the taxi after having paid the driver. While paying the driver she discovered that his breath smelled of liquor. This confirmed her doubts of the driver's character for reasons already given by me to you. She took a sigh of relief that the journey and the lurking fear throughout had ended. What the lady had thought to be the end was just the beginning. She reached home to discover that she had left all the jewellery in the taxi. In the fear of losing the jewellery she had actually lost all the jewellery. She cried and cried for hours and was dead sure that the loss was for good. Meantime the driver reached home and parked the car. While he was checking up whether the four doors of the taxi were locked up, he saw a red coloured bag. He took it home and opened it to see that it contained a lot of jewellery. He felt extremely sorry for the passenger who had lost it. About ten people had travelled in his taxi throughout the day. He could not remember or relate the red bag to its owner. The driver's wife was also as honest as he was. The two discussed how to reach the bag to its owner. The driver could not sleep throughout the night and kept taxing his mind to remember who owned the bag. Eventually he remembered that the last passenger was a lady who was wearing a red coloured dress and carried a red coloured bag. At times matching one's dress with one's bag, belt and shoes can help to match the lost article with its owner. After realising whom the bag belonged to, the driver tried to recall the place where he had left that lady. He was successful in doing so. As soon as he found the answers to all his questions he left for the lady's home. She opened the door with a depressed and defeated facial expression. Her eyes had turned red due to excessive crying. The driver gave the bag to the lady who found all the jewellery to be in tact. Once again she cried but this time the tears were that of joy and not sorrow. She realised that the man about whom she held a bad impression without any reasonable reason had proved himself to be too good. She was also repentant for making presumptions about the driver which were based on suspicion and guess work. It does happen in life that sometimes we do not like a person without any rhyme or reason. Thereafter we find reason(s) to like or even love such a person. After all surprise and change are both synonymous with life. The jewellery was worth Rs 20 lakhs and the taxi driver's honesty was sky-high. The lady built up conversation with the man whom she had feared just a few hours back. During the conversation she discovered that the taxi driver knew about the approximate value of the jewellery. He answered her questions saying that he earned about Rs 3,000 a month and single handedly maintained a family of five people. Life for the poor man who was rich in values was a struggle to make ends meet. The driver said that he did not own the taxi but was running it on behalf of its owner who had to be paid a lion's share of the daily earnings. A person for whom Rs 20 lacs could have been of tremendous materialistic help was too idealistic to keep something that belonged to someone else. The lady was moved by the integrity of the driver and offered him Rs 5,000 as a reward. He did not accept it saying that he had done her no favour but had just answered the call of his conscience. He added that conscience is the presence of God in man and ignoring its call would prove to be disastrous. The lady who had been cheated by all her four own sons on money matters was impressed further by the reply and reaction of the taxi driver. She sold off her old car to the driver for a very friendly price. It was mutually agreed that he would start paying her on easy instalments after he had run the car as his taxi for three years. The lady now had so much of confidence on the man whom she had strongly suspected. The lady said that the car would be handed over after she had done the needful to convert it into a taxi. The delighted driver returned home and informed his wife about the recent developments. Subsequently the taxi was sold and the driver gradually completed the payment process. The lady had also got the driver's wife effectively employed. About five years later the lady died of cancer. She had disinherited all her dishonest sons. The driver who was gratitude personified inherited all her wealth as she had willed it away in his favour. That amounted to Rs 1.5 Crores . This incident would probably be reminding you about the old saying that honesty is the best policy. After all it has been rightly said "As you sow so shall you reap". I hold the view that sometimes people who discard money due to their honesty subsequently see money following them like a shadow.

CHAPTER Eighteen
It Does Not Cost Us Money

To work hard

To think and speak.

To be polite to others.

To be kind to animals.

To be fair in our dealings.

To respect human values.

To encourage the defeated.

To help someone in distress.

To give our share to the poor.

To give good advice to others.

To have confidence in ourselves.

To return something to the owner.

To avoid passing on news that can tarnish someone.

CHAPTER Nineteen
Money and Fear

Because money is dear,
it makes people fear.

In their fear some people cry,
while others even die.

One of the reasons why people desire to possess money is so that they feel secure both in the present and in the future. But once they become moneyed people, they also become insecure. The more they have, the more they are scared of losing what they have. It is for this reason that we can describe money as a double-edged sword.

Quite often one gets to read in the newspapers about various incidents of murder of different people either in the broad daylight or in the dark night. We get to read about kidnapping of people who were held as hostages for ransom. We also hear of bandits looting a rich man's house in his presence. Generally these newspapers are read early in the morning. These tidings send shivers down the spine of many people who dread of sailing in the same boat. Sometimes some people read such news early in the morning and spend the full day in fright and then they can't even sleep a wink at night. Instead of being scared such people should take every care to protect themselves and their money. Their minds should work to find ways and means to ensure that they do not suffer like the people they have read about. Such ways and means include installation of an alarm system in the house, keeping some weapon for their safety, maintaining a watchdog, employing a well-trained guard for the house, taking an insurance cover on the valuables that are kept at home. One such innovative way is to ensure that the lights that are outside the house can be switched on or off from inside the house. This would make prospective thieves realise that the inmates have woken up which would make them run away. Just feeling scared and not exercising due diligence is surely not wise. After all it has been rightly said that God helps those who help themselves.

When we look around us and see how people behave with their money in their fear of losing it we sometimes encounter interesting experiences. A couple comprising of a cagey husband and his fearless wife undertake a train journey while returning from the marriage of the wife's brother. Intermittently during the course of the journey the husband confirms from his wife if all the jewellery is in tact. As using the word jewellery in conversation runs the risk of being overheard by co-passengers, he speaks in code language with his wife. Prior to the commencement of the journey the husband to respond to the code language repeatedly tutors the wife. Time and again the husband asks her how her K is keeping. The word J is purposely not used to rule out the possibility of correct interpretation by eavesdroppers who would interpret J as standing for jewellery. Throughout the night the wife has a sound sleep due to the rocking effect of the train in its motion. On the other hand the husband does not sleep a wink and suspects that some passengers may not be sleeping but pretending to be asleep. His eyeballs keep moving discreetly from left to right and from right to left. He feels that everybody knows everything but the reality remains that everybody knows nothing. After returning from the toilet every time the husband feels the suitcase containing the J. The journey comes to an end and the couple reaches home to discover something to their dismay and disillusion. They realise that their suitcase does not contain the J. It contains only dirty clothes and underclothes, which stink to high hell. A passenger who disembarked from the train at night had willfully replaced the suitcase containing the J with an identical suitcase. Thanks to the husband whose peculiar behaviour had invited the attention of the culprit who had correctly guessed that the couple was carrying valuables. The incident occurred when the train stopped at a station

while the husband was in the toilet. The husband curses the wife for her love for sleep and she curses him for his frequent visits to the toilet. Both the husband and the wife curse the culprit wishing him the worst out of the worst. His dirty clothes are washed by the wife and worn by the husband. That way they recover portion of the cost of the jewellery. After all something is better than nothing.

It has been rightly said that life is a bed of roses with thorns in it. Whenever money comes it can be said that there has been an inflow of flowers. The showers of flowers bring with them a downpour of thorns. While the flowers are always visible as money in its different forms, the thorns are not always visible. Of these thorns, fear is one of them.

CHAPTER Twenty

Beware and Take Care

- Refrain from giving personal financial guarantee.
- Ensure that your financial agreements are well drafted and well documented. Take care that there are clauses and conditions protecting you from the adverse possibilities of the future
- Do not be in a hurry to employ a domestic servant. Before doing so, obtain and verify all relevant information about the prospective servant and preserve his/her photograph.
- Do not be a hurry to get your daughter, sister, niece etc married into a rich family. Ensure that the prospective bridegroom is financially independent.
- While negotiating a financial deal, do not blurt out the monetary consideration you expect. First listen to the amout offered by the other party which could be more than the amount expected by you.
- Before taking out an insurance policy (vehicle/ accident/medical life etc.), find out the duties that are required to be discharged by you in the event of the accident, buglary, fire, hospitalisation, death etc. This would ensure that you do not run helter-skelter on

the occurrence of any space of these eventualities.

- Remember that situations of disaster and crisis provide hunting ground for perperators of fraud.
- Never sign on any paper without reading the contents thereof.
- Never sign a blank cheque or a blank paper.
- Never assign sensitive bank work to others.
- Never act as a custodian of valuables, which are owned by others when you know that you have thieves living with you.
- Never set the combination of your locking devices at 555/420/007/000/123 etc. as these are easy to guess.
- Never discuss financial secrets over the telephone.
- Ensure that your health, house, car and you and not yourself are adequately insured. Remember the dates when such insurance policies are to be renewed.
- Cross check the credentials of an employment agent, especially the ones offering employment overseas, before paying them money.
- Do not divert your attention whenever you deal with cash.
- Do not forget to count money whenever you receive it or pay it.
- Do not forget to make nominations while making investments.

- Do not forget to take back your credit card after having used it.
- Do not leave your credit card number in a hurry after you have finished shopping on the Net.
- Whenever you travel by train, avoid sitting by the side of the window when the train begins to move at a railway platform. This would disable dishonest people from snatching away your money, purse, wallet, chain etc.
- Do not forget the faces of tricksters, which are shown in the media.
- Do not forget what people had told you in respect of your monetary matters. This would disable dishonest people from deceiving or depriving you and your money.
- Do not get duped by buying masterpiece paintings, which though not originals are sold off as originals.
- Note down the key number and the make of the lock that locks up your house, vehicle, safe etc. Ensure that you preserve such data outside your house, vehicle, safe etc.
- Preserve the evidence of payment of rent, telephone bill, electricity bill, school fees, taxes etc. so that you are not required pay these amounts again.
- Make a Will and make more than one copy of it. Preserve these copies in independent locations.

- Make more than one copy of precious financial papers and preserve them in independent locations.
- After using the STD facility on your phone, ensure that you lock up this facility to prevent misuse.
- Ensure that you identify and eliminate hidden costs before you close certain financial deals.
- Ensure that fans, lights, geysers, air-conditioners etc are switched off before you go out of station.
- Ensure that you deposit your cheques, drafts, dividend warrants etc. within the validity period.
- Avoid overspending while on a holiday.
- While travelling out of station or out of the country remember that it is safer to carry travellers' cheques than to carry cash.
- Do not forget to watch the measuring meter of a petrol pump while fuel is being filled into your vehicle. Ensure that the quantity billed is not more than the quantity that has been filled.
- Keep a vigilant watch on your rich husband. Do not let him mingle with shameless ladies. Failure to do so could take away your husband from you.
- Think about the arrival of the worst when you are in the best.
- Take care of your money and your money will take care of you.

CHAPTER Twenty One

Managing Money

Money is the darling of many,
but it also leaves people without a penny.

People have to be careful when they spend,
otherwise they may ask others to lend.

Mismanagement of money makes people broke,
which sometimes gives them a heart stroke.

History bears testimony to the fact that many kings have died as paupers. Managing money is undoubtedly an art. Managing money is even more difficult than earning it. One who is good at earning money need not necessarily be good at managing it. On the other hand, one who is good at managing money need not be good in earning it. It is for this reason that sometimes managers are hired for proper money management and fired for its mismanagement. Monetary discipline should essentially be maintained when one expends money. Failure to do so may result in an irreparable loss. We need to remember that our riches are under the constant threat of becoming history. It is only good money management that can reduce or remove such a risk.

The methodology to be adopted to ensure efficient and effective money management varies from case to case. Where in a particular situation a certain type of expenditure may be imperative, it could be wasteful in another situation. Likewise the priorities of different types of expenditure would be standing in different order in different situations. This is due to the different characters, conditions, constraints, controls, costs etc. that exist in different situations. In addition to this, the consequence(s) flowing due to the postponement or eventual elimination of any particular expenditure varies from environment to environment. The extent, nature and timing of expenditure to be incurred is to be determined keeping in mind several factors. Such factors comprise of both qualitative and quantitative factors. Both the short term and the long term repercussions should be examined and evaluated in terms of importance. Generally the long- term benefits stand in preference to the short-term benefits but then there are certainly exceptions.

The mileage that one shall get by incurring an expenditure should be analysed before incurring it. Expenditure incurred recklessly in a haste results in a waste of resources. While certain types of expenditure are productive in nature, certain types of expenditure are unproductive. Productive expenditure is the one out of which one can get some benefit or the other subsequently which need not be in terms of money. Unproductive expenditure is what we can call meaningless expenditure.

Expenditure that would increase with the passage of time should stand in preference to expenditure, which remains constant in size.

In life sometimes people face a situation when all of a sudden they either get or lose a lot of money. On such occasions they are either excited or depressed. In their excitement or depression they take incorrect monetary decisions. Sometimes when suddenly someone gets a lot of money then people flock around him. At times such people extend invitations to invest funds with them. Subject to the plausibility, monetary decisions should be postponed till the spell of excitement or depression is over. This is for the reason that people are inclined to take incorrect decisions on such occasions. However if the decision cannot wait then one must take the decision. Such decisions should be made by the brain and not by the heart and of course far sightedly and not short sightedly.

The rates of return offered by different investments should be studied and compared. If one is not competent or confident to do so then one must take the assistance of those who are well versed in this field. It pays to speak to more than one person. This way one would probably address important aspects ignored by another. Besides the rate of return, the liquidity factor and the safety factor are also important for anybody investing any amount of money. It is only the combination of their importance, which is different in different circumstances.

Sometimes people possess money but are unable to use

it when it is required. This is an unhappy situation and can be avoided. The different points of time when money shall be needed should be borne in mind while investing the funds. The period for which the funds are invested should match with such requirements. This would ensure that money is available at the required point of time. Likewise the same provision should be made for the amount of money. Sometimes money may be needed in the near future but the exact time cannot be foretold. In such situations the funds must be invested in highly liquid assets which can be encashed any time. Fixed Deposit with a bank is one such financial asset.

In life we do hear of people who have lost a fortune due to some incorrect monetary decision taken by them. One such decision is to lend or invest money for exorbitant returns ignoring the safety of the principal. The tall claims made by leaflets and literature soliciting certain investments mislead people. People get lured away by the empty promises made by money mongers. On the pretext of giving good returns such sinister people sometimes do away with good amount of money. Whenever somebody is promising to give an unusually good return in any monetary deal then the intention is quite questionable. At such times more often than not there is something wrong somewhere. Such crooked people dress up lies with the truth hoping that the lies look like the truth. Sometimes honey flows out of the tongues of such people which is followed by poison flowing out of their hearts. At times such people lay a debt trap which subsequently proves to be a death trap. Here I would like to mention that in respect of money matters people are willing to sacrifice the truth, their relationships and of course their reputation. In such circumstances, though I may sound pessimistic but I feel it is dangerous to place strong confidence on others when it comes to money matters. Though trust is said to be a tradition, this tradition has been broken off and on.

Some people keep yearning for money and keep complaining about their paucity of money. They are unable to find ways and means to make money. Some such people do not study and analyse the returns that they get out of their investments. Some of their investments are either idle or bad. Such investments either get them low returns or no returns. While the bad investments get them poor returns, the idle ones get them no return. The bad investments include shares of companies, which declare poor dividend, real estate fetching low rent etc. The idle investments include jarring jewellery which is worn only on occasions, the terrace of the house owned by them, a plot of land on which they have no intentions of constructing a house, junk shares of companies which declare no dividend etc. Such people should sell off such bad or idle investments. Depending upon their situation, they could either use the sale proceeds thereof or revamp their investment portfolio. They could also resort to a mix of both.

In life we do see people spending money in their

anticipation of getting money in the future. They do so by incurring expenditure that can easily wait till the expected money reaches them. They presume that they will get the expected amount of money at the expected time. Sometimes they get the money they were expecting and sometimes they are disappointed. At times they do get the expected money but not in the quantum it was expected. At times the expected money does not reach them at the expected point of time. This takes them to a liquidity crisis. It is then that such people realise their folly. Such people need to keep a check on their cash flow so that they do not land themselves in a cash crunch. Moreover they need to remember the old adage "There is many a slip between the cup and the lip."

The habit of saving is surely a healthy habit. Our savings are our backbone. Savings give each one of us a feeling of security and stability. It is our savings that help us in the time of need. Our friends may or may not help us during such times but our savings are bound to help us. That umbrella named money is bound to come to our rescue during our rainy days. Whenever our income increases we should increase our savings. Windfall incomes should be wisely invested and not foolishly spent. Those who save regularly make their future secure. We must think of our old age and save. If we do so, we would find sunshine in our sunset days. One does not need to set aside big amounts for a saving. When small sums of money are saved for a long period then the final sum is not small. But for this one needs to start saving early. However, if you have not started saving for the future it is still not late. Remember the saying "Better late than never." By and large the later you start saving, the more is amount required to be set aside.

Some people do not bother to save any money. Such spendthrifts keep wasting their money merrily and recklessly without bothering about their future. They live only in the present forgetting about the future. When the rainy days come due to the gross mismanagement of money by them, then there is nothing available for the present due to their foolish deeds of the past. Generally all the fair weather friends disappear like darkness at the time of dawn and lost time is never found again. The one who does not save is bound to repent. Before we spend we need to remember " Waste not, want not."

Somebody at sometime had advised us not to put all the eggs in one basket. I certainly see an intense meaning in those pearls of wisdom. In the hope of making more and more money people ignore the uncertainties of the future and the effect of external factors over which they probably have no control. The stock market has attracted people towards it by their seeing the illusions of a fantastic future with the help of it. The ebbs and flows of the stock market are easy to witness but difficult to understand. Putting sizeable portion of their wealth in stock market operations and hoping that it multiplies quickly many people have met their downfall. Some people invest their money in only type of financial asset. They should distribute their resources by investing these in different financial assets. Even at the business front, we see people investing uncontrollably into their business without saving for the rainy days. Some businessmen concentrate on only one line of business. They do not even consider the modalities of embarking into another line of business. When the climatic conditions of the business suddenly change due to reasons such as riots, rains, enemy action, price movement, downsliding demand etc. then the past cannot be reversed back. If investments were made in only one type of financial asset, which has proved to be bad, then such investors realise where they went wrong. When such people fall into bad times, they blame lady luck. Actually they are to blame themselves for not having channeled their resources judiciously.

One must necessarily bear in mind the date when an expenditure is to be incurred. On the basis of such dates, one has to ensure that adequate amount of money is available at the right time. Expenses such as payment of rent, electricity, servant's salaries, school/college fees etc are foreseen expenses at the home front. Both the dates of such expenditure and the size thereof are generally known in advance. While preparing the household budget, preference should be given to such unavoidable expenses as against other expenses that can be avoided. On a regular basis some systematic saving should be done for unexpected expenses such as cost of treatment of a sudden illness, cost of tickets for undertaking an unexpected journey, the sudden arrival of outstation guests, the unexpected cost of repairing one's vehicle and such other expenses. Such savings should be invested / deposited in such a way that the same are readily available at the time of need. This would preclude an unhappy situation when money is not available at the time of need. At the time of stocking provisions at home, one should verify the quantities thereof that are already available. This shall not result in a situation when one has accidentally incurred expenditure that could have waited. Old items such as bottles, cans, newspapers etc should be sold off instead of letting such items languish at home. I hope that you would find these tips useful in running your home more judiciously.

The popular saying, which is as old as the hills and speaks of money management, is exceedingly important. As you would have already guessed it is the one, which reminds us of not being penny wise and pound-foolish. Though the saying itself is very old but off and on people have ignored it and eventually realised the depth of its meaning. The realisation has sometimes been done in the nick of time and sometimes after the damage is complete. I feel we must bear this saying in mind whenever we deal with money.

A good money manager does not have to be a money monger though there are some people who hold this incorrect view. A money manager like a manager of any other discipline should have the characteristic of finding remedies for problems and not excuses which can be conveniently called constraints. Anybody who keeps putting excuses one after the other actually helps himself in getting exposed. A good money manager needs to have desirable levels of activeness, boldness, creativity, determination, education, experience, imagination, faithfulness, gratitude, honesty, patience etc. Which of these attributes are required and to what extent depends on the situation. Obviously the attributes mentioned are not exhaustive but merely illustrative. A money manager should be good in the management of men, materials, time, targets etc. This is due to reason of the fact that these factors are to be compulsorily controlled by a manager in any discipline.

When we look at the consequences that good or bad money management can land us in, we begin to ponder. It is then that we reason out the causes that have given birth to such consequences. Scrutinizing and studying the causes can change the consequences desirably.

Good money management could result in increased incomes, luxurious living, prominent people, splendid success, treasure troves and wonderful wives. Bad money management could result in boisterous boys, collapsed confidence, demeaning demotions and fragmented families. Bad money management could also result in lost lovers, poor performance, ravaged reputations and unwanted unhappiness. The outcome that we get out of money management depends on our own doings. Of course external factors over which we have no control certainly have a role to play.

CHAPTER Twenty Two

So Money Goes On ...

During our lifetime we keep listening to different conversations which somehow happen to be related to money. This holds good for both you and me. Different people in different situations with different emotions make such utterances. Have you not heard someone saying..................

- "He has earned money beyond his wildest dreams. His dedication, determination, education, planning and sacrifice have earned him all those laurels."
- We are going for condolence to an extremely rich lady's place. Her husband died a few hours back. I am trying to get you married with her only son who is the heir to all her wealth. If you want to become rich, you must cry bitterly at her place. The more you cry, the more will be the chances of your marrying her son. Even if you don't have tears in your eyes, keep pretending to be wiping them."
- "Your palm says that your husband is having an affair with another woman and going to leave you. Don't feel depressed. A special puja costing Rs. 1,500, can

solve this problem. When should I perform the puja? "

- "He has been tarnishing my reputation. He says all my wealth is tainted and acquired through dubious means. Shamelessly he has been making nasty accusations. All those cock and bull stories are fake, farce, fantasy, fable, fiction and fully fabricated."
- "Why should I be scared of him? No part of his fat salary is being employed in meeting my maintenance expenses."
- " Show me something that is cheaper than this but looks more expensive than this."
- "My grand father could have easily left this house also for us instead of willing it away to charities. God bless him. He must be roaming about as a stray dog in his next birth."
- "People should give the Menu in the Invitation Card. That would facilitate the decision making process of deciding whether to attend or not. "
- "As soon as Mrs Filthy Rich started crying at the death ceremony, ladies

who had finished crying began to cry again. They felt that by doing so she would write their names in her good books."

- "Those who do appear to be rich may not be rich and those who do not appear to be rich could be rich.
- "Though the testimony made by Mr Big Money is undoubtedly untrue, it remains unchallenged, undenied and uncontradicted."
- "Mr Dirty Money is always in the company of Mr Clean Money. He feels that such constant company would remove the dirt from his money."
- "All the efforts of Mr New Money to make friends with Mr Old Money have been a frustrating flop. Thanks to the newness in his money."
- "That dangerous demon named death will not let me remain rich forever."
- "I may not be rich like you but unlike you my youth is still intact. Though I am thirty eight, I don't look a single second older than sweet sixteen."
- " Please get me the check and pack up all this left over food for my puppy dog. Please hurry up, he is waiting for his dinner."
- "He preserves all the presents he gets carefully but distributes them carelessly. On my birthday the foolish fellow presented me the present that I had given him for his birthday two years back."

- "You said that I wasted Rs 150 for this wretched hair cut. I feel that you should not bother your head about my head."
- "All those idle rich people have suddenly become very busy. They are busy disowning their old friend, who is now suddenly engulfed in several money-mongering scandals and is working hard to rescue his reputation. "
- "Next time instead of buying me a present of your choice, you should present me money so that I can buy myself a present of my choice."
- "Sir please do not sack me. My dismissal may give birth to my divorce."
- "Would you be kind, generous and understanding to sanction me the loan at the earliest?"
- "How I wish money grew on trees."
- "And that's how they became rich."

Rs - Dollars - Yen - Pound Sterling